Lecture Notes in Computer Science 12385

More information about this series at http://www.springer.com/series/7407

Dongxiao Yu · Falko Dressler ·
Jiguo Yu (Eds.)

Wireless Algorithms, Systems, and Applications

15th International Conference, WASA 2020
Qingdao, China, September 13–15, 2020
Proceedings, Part II

 Springer

Editors
Dongxiao Yu
Shandong University
Qingdao, China

Falko Dressler
TU Berlin
Berlin, Germany

Jiguo Yu
Qilu University of Technology
Jinan, China

ISSN 0302-9743   ISSN 1611-3349 (electronic)
Lecture Notes in Computer Science
ISBN 978-3-030-59018-5   ISBN 978-3-030-59019-2 (eBook)
https://doi.org/10.1007/978-3-030-59019-2

LNCS Sublibrary: SL1 – Theoretical Computer Science and General Issues

This Springer imprint is published by the registered company Springer Nature Switzerland AG
The registered company address is: Gewerbestrasse 11, 6330 Cham, Switzerland

Preface

The 15th International Conference on Wireless Algorithms, Systems, and Applications (WASA 2020) was held virtually during September 13–15, 2020. The conference focused on new ideas and recent advances in computer systems, wireless networks, distributed applications, and advanced algorithms that are pushing forward the new technologies for better information sharing, computer communication, and universal connected devices in various environments, especially in wireless networks. WASA has become a broad forum for computer theoreticians, system and application developers, and other professionals in networking related areas to present their ideas, solutions, and understandings of emerging technologies and challenges in computer systems, wireless networks, and advanced applications.

The technical program of WASA 2020 consisted of 67 regular papers and 14 short papers, selected by the Program Committee from 216 full submissions in response to the call for papers. All submissions were reviewed by the Program Committee members. These submissions cover many hot research topics, including machine learning algorithms for wireless systems and applications, Internet of Things (IoTs) and related wireless solutions, wireless networking for cyber-physical systems (CPSs), security and privacy solutions for wireless applications, blockchain solutions for mobile applications, mobile edge computing, wireless sensor networks, distributed and localized algorithm design and analysis, wireless crowdsourcing, mobile cloud computing, vehicular networks, wireless solutions for smart cities, wireless algorithms for smart grids, mobile social networks, mobile system security, storage systems for mobile applications, etc. First, we would like to thank all Program Committee members for their hard work in reviewing all submissions. Furthermore, we would like to extend our special thanks to the WASA Steering Committee for their consistent leadership and guidance; we also would like to thank the the local chairs (Prof. Feng Li and Prof. Jianbo Li), the publication chairs (Prof. Wei Li, Prof. Yi Liang, and Prof. Xiao Zhang), the publicity chair (Prof. Yanwei Zheng) and the Web chairs (Dr. Cheng Zhang, Dr. Qi Luo, and Dr. Jinfeng Dou) for their hard work in making WASA 2020 a success. In particular, we would like to thank all the authors for submitting and presenting their exciting ideas and solutions at the conference.

August 2020

Xiuzhen Cheng
Yinglong Wang
Dongxiao Yu
Falko Dressler
Jiguo Yu

Organization

Steering Committee Members

Xiuzhen Susan Cheng (Co-chair)	The George Washington University, USA
Zhipeng Cai (Co-chair)	Georgia State University, USA
Jiannong Cao	Hong Kong Polytechnic University, Hong Kong, China
Ness Shroff	The Ohio State University, USA
Wei Zhao	University of Macau, Macau, China
PengJun Wan	Illinois Institute of Technology, USA
Ty Znati	University of Pittsburgh, USA
Xinbing Wang	Shanghai Jiao Tong University, China

General Co-chairs

Yinglong Wang	Qilu University of Technology, China
Xiuzhen Cheng	Shandong University, China

Program Co-chairs

Dongxiao Yu	Shandong University, China
Falko Dressler	University of Paderborn, Germany
Jiguo Yu	Qilu University of Technology, China

Publicity Co-chair

Yanwei Zheng	Shandong University, China

Publication Co-chairs

Wei Li	Georgia State University, USA
Yi Liang	Georgia State University, USA
Xiao Zhang	Shandong University, China

Local Co-chairs

Feng Li	Shandong University, China
Jianbo Li	Qingdao University, China

Web Co-chairs

Cheng Zhang	The George Washington University, USA
Qi Luo	Shandong University, China
Jinfeng Dou	Shandong University, China

Program Committee

Ashwin Ashok	Georgia State University, USA
Yu Bai	California State University Fullerton, USA
Ran Bi	Dalian University of Technology, China
Edoardo Biagioni	University of Hawaii at Manoa, USA
Salim Bitam	University of Biskra, Algeria
Azzedine Boukerche	SITE, Canada
Zhipeng Cai	Georgia State University, USA
Sriram Chellappan	University of South Florida, USA
Changlong Chen	Microsoft, USA
Fei Chen	Shenzhen University, China
Quan Chen	Guangdong University of Technology, China
Songqing Chen	George Mason University, USA
Xianfu Chen	VTT Technical Research Centre of Finland, Finland
Yingwen Chen	National University of Defense Technology, China
Siyao Cheng	Harbin Institute of Technology, China
Soufiene Djahel	Manchester Metropolitan University, UK
Yingfei Dong	University of Hawaii, USA
Zhuojun Duan	James Madison University, USA
Luca Foschini	University of Bologna, Italy
Jing Gao	Dalian University of Technology, China
Xiaofeng Gao	Shanghai Jiao Tong University, China
Sukhpal Singh Gill	Queen Mary University of London, UK
Daniel Graham	University of Virginia, USA
Meng Han	Kennesaw State University, USA
Zaobo He	Miami University, USA
Pengfei Hu	VMWare Inc., USA
Qiang-Sheng Hua	Huazhong University of Science and Technology, China
Baohua Huang	Guangxi University, China
Yan Huang	Kennesaw State University, USA
Yan Huo	Beijing Jiaotong University, China
Holger Karl	University of Paderborn, Germany
Donghyun Kim	Georgia State University, USA
Hwangnam Kim	Korea University, South Korea
Abderrahmane Lakas	UAE University, UAE
Sanghwan Lee	Kookmin University, South Korea
Feng Li	IUPUI, USA
Feng Li	Shandong University, China

Contents – Part II

Contents – Part I

Short Papers

Cluster-Based Basic Safety Message Dissemination in VANETs

Lin Chen[1,2], Xiaoshuang Xing[1(✉)], Gaofei Sun[1(✉)], Jiang Xu[1], and Jie Zhang[1]

[1] School of Computer Science and Engineering,
Changshu Institute of Technology, Suzhou, China
20185227092@stu.suda.edu.cn, {xing,gfsun}@cslg.edu.cn,
153204277@qq.com, 1700117425@qq.com
[2] School of Computer Science and Technology, Soochow University, Suzhou, China

Abstract. Vehicles in the vehicular ad-hoc networks (VANETs) share traffic information by broadcasting basic safety messages (BSMs) which helps improve traffic efficiency and safety. With the increase of traffic density, more BSMs will be broadcasted and collisions will occur frequently. Based on the fact that BSMs broadcasted by nearby vehicles contain similar traffic information, we propose a cluster-based BSMs dissemination scheme in this paper. Nearby vehicles form a cluster with the vehicle that maintains relative stable distance with others being the cluster header. The cluster headers broadcast the BSMs on behalf of the cluster members and intersected members belonging to multiple clusters help relaying BSMs among clusters. Simulation results show that the method proposed in this paper can effectively reduce the number of broadcasted BSMs. The transmission collisions are reduced and the successful BSM transmission ratio is significantly improved through our design.

Keywords: BSM dissemination · Clustering · CSMA/CA · VANETs

1 Introduction

The rapid increase in the number of vehicles caused a series of social problems such as anabatic traffic congestion and traffic accidents [1]. VANET has been considered as a promising solution to these problems [2]. Vehicles in VANETs share traffic information via broadcasting BSMs thus improve traffic efficiency and safety. BSM dissemination plays a critical role on the performance of the VANETs.

Dedicated short range communication (DSRC) [4] is one of the commonly adopted protocols in VANETs communication. According to DSRC, the time is divided into 100 ms time periods. Each time period is further divided into two slots namely time slot 0 and time slot 1. Time slot 0 is 50 ms long and it is reserved for BSMs broadcasting on one control channel (CCH). Time slot 1 is 50 ms long and it is reserved for other communications among vehicles on six service channels (SCHs). As all vehicles broadcast BSMs within 50 ms on the

© Springer Nature Switzerland AG 2020
D. Yu et al. (Eds.): WASA 2020, LNCS 12385, pp. 3–10, 2020.
https://doi.org/10.1007/978-3-030-59019-2_1

same CCH, collisions occur frequently especially in high traffic density scenarios [3,5]. Collisions on the BSM dissemination will lead to long BSMs transmission delay and even failure BSMs transmission which will affect the performance of the VANETs. To deal with this problem, efforts have been made on the optimization of BSM dissemination from different aspects. Efficient BSM dissemination schemes have been proposed by reducing the transmission frequency and adjusting the transmission power [6–8]. However, the performance improvement of these schemes is limited in high traffic denseity scenarios [9]. When vehicles are congested on the road, the distance among vehicles is small and the traffic information contained in the BSMs broadcasted by nearby vehicles will be similar. Therefore, numerous redundant BSMs containing similar traffic information will be transmitted on the CCH in dense VANETs. To further improve the BSM dissemination efficiency in high traffic density scenarios, cluster-based methods have been proposed. In [10], vehicles are clustered based upon their mobility which is mainly related to the speed. Vehicles in one cluster have similar velocity. After clustering, different channel accessing priorities are assigned to clusters according to the speed of the clusters to optimize the bandwidth utilization. [11] introduced a novel dynamic mobility-based clustering scheme for VANETs. The clusters are formed based on vehicles' mobility patterns, including moving direction, relative velocity, relative distance, and link lifetime. This scheme performs well in terms of the stability of the formed clusters since the lifetime of the link is taken into consideration. [12] proposed a multi-hop clustering scheme based on the relative mobility. The stability of the clusters is also considered in the design. However, these existing works mainly focus on designing the cluster formation schemes, maintaining the stability of the clusters, and selecting proper cluster headers. Few efforts have been made on designing the BSM dissemination scheme after clusters are formed. It is still an open issue to design the message format for cluster-based BSM dissemination and define the dissemination rules to be followed by the cluster headers and the cluster members. In this paper, we deal with these issues and the contributions are summarized as follows:

1. A cluster formation algorithm is designed based on the relative mobility of vehicles. Considering the varying driving state of vehicles, we propose that all vehicles can re-cluster after a time period of T.
2. We propose a novel cluster-based BSM dissemination scheme. Two message formats are defined for BSM dissemination and the dissemination rules are designed for cluster headers, cluster members, and intersected cluster members.
3. Extensive simulation study is conducted to validate the performance of our design. Results show that the number of broadcasted BSMs is reduced, less transmission collisions occur on the CCH, and the successful transmission ratio is significantly improved.

The rest of the paper is organized as following. Section 2 describes the system model and the problem to be solved. The cluster formation algorithm and the cluster-based BSM dissemination scheme are designed in Sect. 3 and Sect. 4

respectively. Simulation results are analyzed in Sect. 5 and we conclude the paper in Sect. 6.

2 System Model and Problem Description

There are N vehicles denoted by $V = \{1, 2, \ldots, N\}$ in a VANET. According to the DSRC protocol [4], each vehicle broadcasts BSMs 10 times per second on the CCH. The BSM contains information about the location of the vehicle, the moving speed, the acceleration, the moving direction, and the traffic information around. Traffic information may include the traffic light state, lane information, the traffic congestion level, and other information that helps improve traffic efficiency and safety [13]. In high traffic density scenarios, vehicles are congested on the road and the distance among vehicles is small. In this case, the traffic information contained in the BSMs broadcasted by nearby vehicles will be similar. Redundant information will be transmitted on the CCH leading to frequent transmission collisions, low success transmission ratio, and long transmission delay.

In this paper, we aim at reliving the aforementioned problems by proposing a cluster-based BSM dissemination scheme. m clusters, denoted by $CL = \{c_1, c_2, \ldots, c_m\}$, will be formed for N vehicles. Each cluster $c_i, i \in \{1, 2, \cdots, m\}$ consists of one cluster header and n_i cluster members. It can be denoted by $c_i = \{H_i, M_i^1, M_i^2, \ldots, M_i^{n_i}\}$ with $H_i \in V$ being the cluster header and $M_i^k \in V, k \in \{1, 2, \cdots, n_i\}$ being one cluster member. For any two clusters c_i and c_j, $i \neq j$, there are two cases. Let $c_i \cap c_j = c_{ij}$, c_i and c_j are called as independent clusters if $c_{ij} = \varnothing$. Otherwise, c_i and c_j are called as intersected clusters and any $M_i^k \in c_{ij}$ is called as an intersected member. Once clusters are formed, they will last for a time duration of T such that reduce the time and other resource wasted for frequent re-clustering. Within T, each cluster header will broadcast BSMs as a representative of the cluster while cluster members except for the intersected members will keep silent. Intersected members will act as relays helping on information exchange among clusters. Through this way, the number of broadcasted BSMs containing similar information will be reduced. Therefore, transmission collisions will be reduced and BSMs can be shared more efficiently. In the following two sections, we will design the cluster formation algorithm and propose a cluster-based BSM dissemination scheme.

3 Cluster Formation Algorithm

Clusters must be formed before conducting the cluster-based BSM dissemination. Recall the discussion in Sect. 2, nearby vehicles will generate BSMs containing similar information. Therefore, vehicles that are close to each other can form a cluster to avoid redundant BSMs broadcasting. Besides, once a cluster is formed it will last for a time duration of T. The distance among the cluster members and the cluster header should keep short within T in order to make sure that the cluster header is always a good representative of the cluster for BSMs broadcasting. Based on these considerations, we take the distance between vehicles at the current time and the distance between vehicles after T as the main indicators when forming clusters and choosing cluster headers.

Let $i, j \in V$ be two vehicles. Before clusters are formed, they broadcast BSMs containing information about their locations, moving speed, acceleration, and moving directions, independently. Once received the BSMs broadcasted by each other, i and j can easily calculate the Euclidian distance between them at the current time, denoted by d_{ij}, and the expected Euclidian distance between them after T, denoted by d'_{ij}. If $d_{ij} \leq R$ and $d'_{ij} \leq R$, they will call each other as a neighbor. Here, R is a predefined neighboring radius. Each vehicle will only be able to form clusters with its neighbors, therefore R will affect the size of the clusters. Let $N_i = \{i_1, i_2, \ldots, i_{max_i}\}$ denote the set of vehicle i's neighbors. i will calculate the change of the distance between it and any neighbor $j \in N_i$ within T as

$$mov_{ij} = \left| d_{ij} - d'_{ij} \right|. \tag{1}$$

Taking the average of all the neighbors, i will get

$$mov_i = \sum_{j=i_1}^{i_{max_i}} mov_{ij}/max_i, \tag{2}$$

A small mov_i indicates that vehicle i stay close with its neighbors and the distance between i and its neighbors is relatively stable within T. Therefore, a vehicle with smaller mov_i should be a better option to act as the cluster header. To make sure that vehicles with small mov_i will be selected as the cluster headers, we define a fallback timer T_i (in ms) as

$$T_i = mov_i/2R \times 50, \tag{3}$$

Here, $2R$ is the upper bound of mov_i. 50 ms is the time length of one slot 0, which is reserved for BSM broadcasting according to the DSRC protocol. Once obtained T_i, vehicle i will wait for a time duration of T_i then it will broadcast a CH_I message together with its public key (NK_i, PK_i) indicating that i will become a cluster header. Any neighbor $j \in N_i$ receiving CH_I and (NK_i, PK_i) will become a cluster member of vehicle i. The neighbor will withdraw its fallback timer and save the received public key (NK_i, PK_i) in a list L_j. $|L_j| = 1$ indicates that vehicle j is a cluster member of only one cluster and $|L_j| = k \geq 2$ indicates that j is an intersected member of k clusters. Through this way, clusters are formed. Each time T passes, the clusters will be reformed in a same way.

4   Cluster-Based BSM Dissemination Scheme

After the formation of clusters, the cluster headers can be used to broadcast BSMs on behalf of the clusters during each T. In order to enable BSMs information sharing among clusters and ensure that the BSMs can be received by wider range of vehicles, intersected members are explored to act as relays.

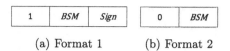

(a) Format 1　　　(b) Format 2

Fig. 1. BSM broadcasting formats

Algorithm 1: Cluster-based BSM Dissemination

For any cluster header H_i receiving a BSM
if *the indicator bit is '1' or* $BSM \in BSM_{H_i}$ **then**
  | H_i discards the BSM message
else
  | H_i broadcasts the BSM in Format 1
end
For any cluster member j with $|L_j| = 1$ receiving a BSM
if *the indicator bit is '1' and* $(NK, PK) \in L_j$ *and* $h(BSM) = Sign^{PK}$
  mod NK **then**
  | j decodes the BSM message for traffic information
else
  | j discards the BSM message
end
For any intersected member j with $|L_j| \geq 2$ receiving the BSM
if *the indicator bit is '0' or* $BSM \in BSM_j$ **then**
  | j discards the BSM message
else if $\exists (NK, PK) \in L_j$ *such that* $h(BSM) = Sign^{PK}$ mod NK **then**
  | j decodes the BSM message for traffic information and j broadcasts the
  | BSM in Format 2
end

For each cluster c_i, its cluster header H_i maintains two lists. One list Key_{H_i} saves a pair of public key and secret key, it is denoted by $Key_{H_i} = ((NK_i, PK_i), (NK_i, SK_i))$. (NK_i, PK_i) has been broadcasted to the cluster members of c_i during the cluster formation process. The other list BSM_{H_i} saves the BSMs that have been broadcasted by H_i within the current T, it is denoted as $BSM_{H_i} = \{BSM_{H_i}^1, BSM_{H_i}^2, \cdots\}$. For each intersected member j, it maintains two lists. One list L_j saves the public keys of the cluster headers of those clusters that j belongs to. The other list BSM_j saves the BSMs that have been relayed by j within the current T, it is denoted as $BSM_j = \{BSM_j^1, BSM_j^2, \cdots\}$. For each cluster member other than the intersected members, it only saves the the public key of its cluster header. Two BSM broadcasting formats, namely Format 1 and Format 2, are defined for the cluster header and the intersected members respectively. A Format 1 BSM broadcasted by a cluster header H_i is given in Fig. 1(a). The first digit is called as the indicator bit, with '1' indicating that the message is broadcasted by a cluster header. BSM is the BSM message and $Sign$ is the signature of the cluster header which can be calculated as

$$Sign = h(BSM)^{SK_{H_i}} \mod NK_{H_i} \tag{4}$$

Here, $h(\cdot)$ is the hash function. A Format 2 BSM broadcasted by an intersected member is given in Fig. 1(b). The indicator bit equals to '0' indicates that the message is broadcasted by an intersected member. BSM is the BSM message. Based on the defined lists and formats, the cluster-based BSM dissemination scheme is given in Algorithm 1.

5 Performance Evaluation

In this section we validate the performance of our design through simulation study carried out in MATLAB. First, we investigate the affects of the traffic density and the neighboring radius R on the number of clusters formed using our cluster formation algorithm. The traffic density is defined as the number of vehicles on a lane of one kilometer at one instant. We conduct simulation in a one kilometer barrier-free two-way road. The location, speed, and acceleration of the vehicles are randomly generated. Then clusters are formed according to the cluster formation algorithm designed in Sect. 3. The simulation results are given in Fig. 2(a). It is obvious that more clusters will be formed for higher density traffic scenarios and less clusters will be formed for larger R. Figure 2(b) shows the number of broadcasted BSMs within 50 ms for different traffic density and R. Higher density or smaller R will lead to more clusters thus larger number of BSMs will be broadcasted. Moreover, it can be found that the number of BSMs broadcasted after clustering is significantly less than the number of BSMs broadcasted before clustering.

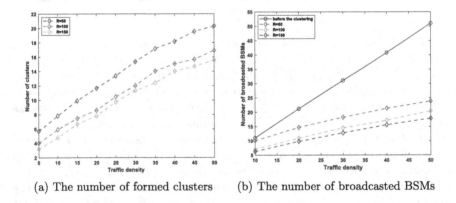

(a) The number of formed clusters   (b) The number of broadcasted BSMs

Fig. 2. Performance of the cluster formation algorithm

We further investigate the performance of the cluster-based BSM dissemination scheme from the perspective of the number of collisions occurred within 50 ms and the transmission success ratio of the broadcasted BSMs. The simulation environments are set according to IEEE 802.11. That is, vehicles contend for broadcasting BSMs on the CCH according to the CSMA/CA protocol. The simulation parameters are set as listed in Table 1. The simulation results are shown in Fig. 3. It can be found that compared with traditional non-clustering BSM dissemination schemes, the proposed cluster-based scheme can significantly reduce the number of collisions and improve the successful transmission ratio especially when the traffic density is high. Besides, the increase of CW will lead to increased number of collisions and decreased successful transmission ratio. The reason is that less contention opportunities will be provided during 50 ms when CW gets greater. This will lead to more contentions for each opportunity and thus more collisions and less success ratio. When NB gets larger, a vehicle will try more times to get access to the CCH. Therefore, more contentions and collisions will occur, and the successful transmission ratio will go lower.

Table 1. Simulation parameters setting

Parameter	Meaning	Value
R	Neighboring radius	50 m, 100 m, 150 m
CW	Competition window	1, 2
NB	Maximum number of backoff	3, 4

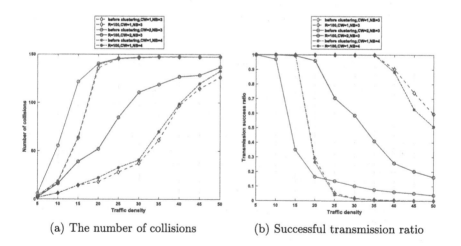

(a) The number of collisions   (b) Successful transmission ratio

Fig. 3. Performance of the cluster-based BSM dissemination scheme

6   Conclusion

This paper enhances the performance of BSM dissemination in VANETs by proposing a cluster formation algorithm and a cluster-based BSM dissemination scheme. Simulation results show that our design can reduce the number of BSMs broadcasted on the CCH, transmission collisions are reduced and the successful transmission ratio of the BSMs is significantly improved. In our future work, we will further investigate the accuracy of cluster-based BSM dissemination. That is the deviation between the BSMs broadcasted by the cluster header and the BSMs broadcasted by a cluster member itself.

Acknowledgement. The authors would like to thank the support from the Natural Science Foundation of China (61702056, 61602062), CERNET Innovation Project (NGII20161002), the Natural Science Foundation of Jiangsu Province (BK20191475), and the Qing Lan Project of Jiangsu Province (No. 2019).

References

1. Wang, J., Cai, Z., Yu, J.: Achieving personalized k-anonymity-based content privacy for autonomous vehicles in CPS. IEEE Trans. Ind. Inform. **16**(6), 4242–4251 (2020)
2. Sakiz, F., Sen, S.: A survey of attacks and detection mechanisms on intelligent transportation systems: VANETs and IoV. Ad Hoc Netw. **61**, 33–50 (2017)
3. Guan, X., Huang, Y., Cai, Z., Ohtsuki, T.: Intersection-based forwarding protocol for vehicular ad hoc networks. Telecommun. Syst. **62**(1), 67–76 (2016)
4. S. S. J. S. I. D. Committee et al.: Dedicated short range communications (DSRC) message set dictionary. SAE International (2016)
5. Liu, L., Chen, C., Qiu, T., Zhang, M., Li, S., Zhou, B.: A data dissemination scheme based on clustering and probabilistic broadcasting in VANETs. Veh. Commun. **13**, 78–88 (2018)
6. Goudarzi, F., Asgari, H.: Non-cooperative beacon power control for VANETs. IEEE Trans. Intell. Transp. Syst. **20**(2), 777–782 (2018)
7. Liu, B., Jia, D., Wang, J., Lu, K., Wu, L.: Cloud-assisted safety message dissemination in VANET-cellular heterogeneous wireless network. IEEE Syst. J. **11**(1), 128–139 (2017)
8. Cai, Z., Zheng, X.: A private and efficient mechanism for data uploading in smart cyber-physical systems. IEEE Trans. Netw. Sci. Eng. **7**(2), 766–775 (2020)
9. Cai, Z., Zheng, X., Yu, J.: A differential-private framework for urban traffic flows estimation via taxi companies. IEEE Trans. Ind. Inform. **15**(12), 6492–6499 (2019)
10. Gupta, N., Prakash, A., Tripathi, R.: Clustering based cognitive mac protocol for channel allocation to prioritize safety message dissemination in vehicular ad-hoc network. Veh. Commun. **5**, 44–54 (2016)
11. Ren, M., Khoukhi, L., Labiod, H., Zhang, J., Veque, V.: A mobility-based scheme for dynamic clustering in vehicular ad-hoc networks (VANETs). Veh. Commun. **9**, 233–241 (2017)
12. Azizian, M., Cherkaoui, S., Hafid, A.S.: A distributed D-hop cluster formation for VANET. In: IEEE Wireless Communications and Networking Conference, pp. 1–6. IEEE (2016)
13. Xiong, Z., Li, W., Han, Q., Cai, Z.: Privacy-preserving auto-driving: a GAN-based approach to protect vehicular camera data. In: IEEE International Conference on Data Mining, pp. 668–677 (2019)

On-Road Vehicle Detection Algorithm Based on Mathematical Morphology

Wei Chen[1,2], Zusheng Zhang[2(✉)], Xiaoling Wu[1], and Jianguang Deng[2]

[1] Department of Computer Science,
Guangdong University of Technology, Guangzhou 510090, China
[2] School of Cyberspace Security, Dongguan University of Technology,
Dongguan 523808, China
zszhang@dgut.edu.cn

Abstract. Wireless magnetic sensor network is gradually used in the intelligent traffic detection system. However, the magnetic sensor is susceptible to the geomagnetic interference. The operation of electric railway systems, such as subways and light rail systems, generates geomagnetic interference signal. Most existing detection systems are prone to high false detection rates in the case of interference environment. This work proposes an on-road vehicle detection algorithm which can effectively eliminate interference signal. Based on mathematical morphology, we designed two filters for extracting the signals of moving and static vehicles from interfered magnetic signals. We have deployed an experiment system at the intersection nearby a subway. Experiment results show that the algorithm has an accuracy rate of more than 98% for vehicle detection.

Keywords: Vehicle detection · Magnetic sensor · Interference · Morphological filter

1 Introduction

Currently, ITS (Intelligent Transportation System) has attracted the attention of many researchers because it is an effective way to solve urban traffic congestion [1]. Vehicle detection system provides basis data for ITS, and it is an important part of ITS.

There are many vehicle detection technologies, such as: inductive loop [2], camera [3], microwave radar [4], etc. The installation and maintenance of inductive loop is expensive. Microwave radar is easily affected by the environment. The camera is susceptible to shadows and bad weather. Wireless magnetic sensor network is immune to the effects of environmental factors such as rain, wind and

This work was supported in part by the National Natural Science Fund, China (No. 61872083), in part by the projects of Guangdong Province (No. 2019A151501 1123 and 2018KTSCX221), and in part by the innovative service project (No. 2019ZYF WXFD02).

D. Yu et al. (Eds.): WASA 2020, LNCS 12385, pp. 11–19, 2020.
https://doi.org/10.1007/978-3-030-59019-2_2

snow, and it has the advantages of low cost, low power consumption, small size. Recently, the magnetic sensor-based traffic detection system has been present in both the research community and industry.

Cheung et al. [5] studied the vehicle detection and speed estimation using magnetic sensor. Chen et al. [6] designed a vehicle classification method based on wireless sensor network. Qiao et al. [7] used magnetic sensors to detect the distance change between the axle and the frame to check the vehicle load. Bo Yang [8] designed a vehicle detection algorithm in the low-speed environment of urban traffic. In refer [9], our group proposed an anti-interference traffic speed estimation system with wireless magnetic sensor network. However, the algorithm is not suitable for vehicle detection at intersections. The algorithm in this work is an improvement on the basis of refer [9].

The magnetic sensor is susceptible to geomagnetic interference. The operation of electrified railway systems, such as subways and light rails, produce interference magnetic signal. Lowes [10] found that the magnetic field interference mainly caused by the track leakage current and the high voltage power line. Pirjola et al. [11] proposed a calculation model for the magnetic field generated by direct current railways.

Most of the existing algorithms don't consider the magnetic interference problem. They are susceptible to the magnetic interference and result in high false and missed detection rates. This work proposes a vehicle detection algorithm which can remove magnetic interference. Based on the mathematical morphology, we designed two filters to extract the magnetic signal of vehicles. Experiment results show that the accuracy of the proposed algorithm is 98%, which is better than the existing algorithms.

The remainder of this paper is organized as follows. Section 2 describes problem definition. Section 3 proposes the algorithm for vehicle detection at intersection. Section 4 conducts experiments to prove the performance of the algorithm. Finally, Sect. 5 makes a brief conclusion.

2   Problem Definition

Figure 1(a) shows the diagram of the electric railway system. The traction station is to supply DC traction power in a certain section. The feeder line is used to transport DC power to the contact rail. Due to the contact between the rail and the ground, the stray current in the rail will leak to the ground to form a leakage current.

The train itself and the traction station also generate magnetic interference, but the influence on the magnetic sensor nodes on the surface can be ignored. The interference signal of magnetic field is mainly caused by the leakage current from the rail to earth [12]. Figure 1(b) shows the interference signal which is collected by a magnetic sensor near a subway station.

Sensor node is deployed in each lane of the intersection. When the signal light is green, the vehicles pass through the sensor node in turn. When the signal light is red, the vehicle arriving at the intersection stops on the sensor node

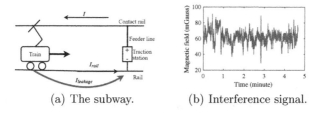

(a) The subway. (b) Interference signal.

Fig. 1. Magnetic interference from the subway. (Color figure online)

and waits for the green light. Therefore, the vehicle detection at an intersection includes moving vehicle detection and static vehicle detection. The vehicle detection problem at an intersection can be defined as:

Vehicle detection: $s(i) = Vehicle\_detection(M_j(i))$
Input: the signal $M(i)$ collected by magnetic sensor

$$M_j(i) = V_j(i) + E_j(i) + G_j(i) \quad j \in \{x, y, z\} \tag{1}$$

where i is the sampling sequence number, V is the vehicle magnetic signal, E is the earth's magnetic field, G is the interference magnetic signal, j is the index of sensor's x, y, and z axes.

Task: The algorithm needs to eliminate the geomagnetic interference signal, and to detect the characteristics of magnetic signal caused by moving vehicle and static vehicle.

Output:
$s(i)= 1$: there has a vehicle passing or stop on the sensor node.
$s(i)= 0$: the sensor node does not detect a vehicle.

3 Algorithm of Vehicle Detection

The overall architecture of the proposed algorithm is illustrated in Fig. 2. The sampled signal is input to two filters: 1) The Gaussian structure morphology filter is used to detect the moving vehicles; 2) The rectangular structure morphology filter is used to detect the temporary stopped vehicles which are waiting signal light. Final, the output results of the two filters are combined to get the traffic flow.

The experimental data shows that the x and z axis signals change significantly when a vehicle is on the sensor node, while the y axis changes less. If vehicle detection only based on the signal of a single axis, it is easy to cause false detection. So the x and z axis signals are selected for synthesis, as shown in Eq. (2).

$$D(i) = \sqrt{M_y^2(i) + M_z^2(i)} \tag{2}$$

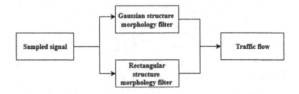

Fig. 2. The flowchart of algorithm

3.1   Moving Vehicle Detection

When a vehicle passes through the magnetic sensor, the waveform of magnetic signal collected by the sensor node is fluctuate up and down. As shown in Fig. 3(a), the fluctuation of the signal generated by the vehicle is larger than that of the magnetic interference signal. The fused signal $D(i)$ is transformed into variance sequence $Var(i)$, as shown in Fig. 3(b).

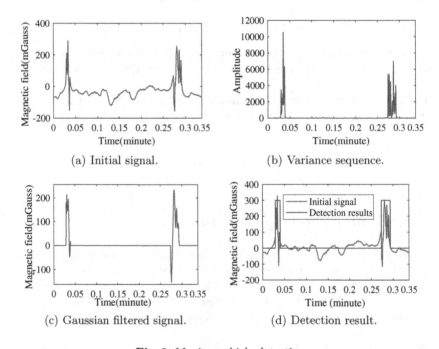

Fig. 3. Moving vehicle detection.

As shown in Eq. (3), Given a threshold H_{Th}, the signal segments of the suspected vehicle signal can be extracted from the input signal. Then, the extracted signal is filtered by a morphology filter to determine whether it is a vehicle signal.

$$F(i) = \begin{cases} D(i) & if \quad Var(i) \geq H_{Th} \\ 0 & if \quad Var(i) < H_{Th} \end{cases} \tag{3}$$

The morphological filter to extract the signal of moving vehicle is shown as the Eq. (4), where $F(i)$ is the input signal, $g(m)$ is the structural element, $OC = F \circ g \bullet g$ is the open and close operation, and $CO = F \bullet g \circ g$ is the close and open operation. The details of opening and closing operations are described in the refer [13]. The operation of OC can eliminate the peak (positive pulse). The operation of CO is used to eliminate troughs (negative pulses).

$$y_1(i) = (OC(F(i), g(m)) + CO(F(i), g(m)))/2 \qquad (4)$$

The waveform of magnetic signal caused by a moving vehicle is the Gaussian-like structure [9]. The filter needs to remove interference and retain the characteristics of the vehicle signal, so the Gaussian function is selected to construct the morphological structure elements as the Eq. (5),

$$g(m) = \frac{P}{\sqrt{2\pi\sigma^2}} e^{-\frac{(m-L/2)^2}{2\sigma^2}} \quad 0 \le m \le L \qquad (5)$$

where P is an amplification factor, σ is the variance, and L is the length of the structural element. For example, Fig. 3(a) is the initial signal $D(i)$. Figure 3(c) is output of the filtered, and Fig. 3(d) is the result of the binary detection of the input signal enlarged by 1: 300.

3.2   Static Vehicle Detection

The morphological filter to extract the signal of static vehicle is shown as the Eq. (6), where $D(i)$ is the input signal, $h(n)$ is the structural element.

$$y_2(i) = (OC(D(i), h(n)) + CO(D(i), h(n)))/2 \qquad (6)$$

At an intersection, a static vehicle is a vehicle that stops on a sensor node and waits for a green light. The magnetic signal of static vehicle is a rectangular-like signal, as shown in Fig. 4(a). Therefore, using rectangular structure element $h(n) = H \, 1 \le n \le W$ to filter the signal, where H is a constant, W is the length of structural elements.

The magnetic signals created by electric railway contain positive and negative pulse. In order to remove interference, W must greater than the width of pulses. There is also a limit to the upper of W. Assume that the stopping time of the vehicle is $T_{stopping}$, then the length of the rectangle signal to be extracted is $W_{stopping} = T_{stopping} * f$, f is the sampling frequency. If $W > W_{stopping}$, the target rectangle signal will be filtered out as noise, so $W_{max} < Minimum(W_{stopping})$. Usually, the height of the structural element H has no effect on the performance of the filter, so a constant value is taken. For example, the results of the rectangular structure morphology filtering is shown in Fig. 4(b), and Fig. 4(c) is the result of the binary detection of the input signal enlarged by 1: 300.

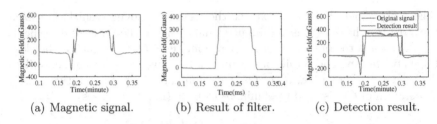

(a) Magnetic signal.   (b) Result of filter.   (c) Detection result.

Fig. 4. Static vehicle detection.

3.3 Pseudo Code of Algorithm

Gaussian and rectangular filters can detect moving and static vehicles respectively. So vehicle detection algorithm at an intersection is fusion the output of these two filters. The pseudo code of MFDA (Morphological filter detection algorithm) is shown in Algorithm 1.

Algorithm 1: MFDA Algorithm

---
1 Function $S(i) = Vehicle\_detection(M_j(i))$
   Input : The original samples $M_j(i)$ $j \in \{x, y, z\}$
   Output: s(i)=0, no vehicle; s(i)=1, a vehicle.
2 $D(i) \leftarrow \{M_y(i), M_z(i)\}$;/* Signal synthesis   */
3 $Var(i) \leftarrow D(i)$; /* Variance   */
4 $F(i) \leftarrow \{Var(i), D(i)\}$;/* Extract vehicle signals   */
5 $y_1(i) = (OC(F(i), g(m)) + CO(F(i), g(m))) / 2$;
6 $B_1(i) = Binarize(y_1(i), A_1)$;
7 $y_2(i) = (OC(D(i), h(n)) + CO(D(i), h(n))) / 2$;
8 $B_2(i) = Binarize(y_2(i), A_2)$;
9 **if** $(B_1(i) == 1 \ or \ B_2(i) == 1)$ **then**
10 | $s(i) = 1$;
11 **else**
12 | $s(i) = 0$;
13 **end**

---

4 Experiment

In order to test the vehicle detection algorithm, we conducted experiments at the intersection near the Keyuan subway station, Shenzhen, China. As shown in Fig. 5(a), the sensor node uses STM8L151C8 MCU, with LoRa SX1278 communication module, integrated HMC5883L magnetic sensor. The node runs the Contiki operating system [14] and its shell uses a high-strength PC material for resisting the weight of vehicles. The routers and BS use wireless communication and are solar powered. As shown in Fig. 5(b), each of router and BS is equipped with a 44 Ah lithium battery pack and a solar panel. The routers and BS are attached on roadside lampposts to improve the quality of wireless communication and solar charging efficiency. The values of experimental parameters are shown in Table 1.

(a) Sensor node   (b) BS

Fig. 5. The sensor node and BS.

Table 1. The experimental parameter values

Parameters	Description	Value
p	The Magnification factor of Gaussian structure	450
σ	Variance of Gaussian structure element	4.2
L	The length of Gaussian structure element	19
W	The width of rectangular structure element	25
A_1	The binary threshold of Gaussian signal	20
A_2	The binary threshold of rectangular signal	50

In order to verify the performance of the algorithm, we compare the detection results with the adaptive threshold algorithm (ATA) [5], fixed threshold algorithm for short term variance sequence (SVA) [8] and double-window detection algorithm for variance sequence (DVA) [15]. The accuracy of ATA, SVA and DVA are 75%, 90% and 92% respectively, as shown in Table 2.

Figure 6(a) is the initial signal, which includes the vehicle signal, the magnetic interference signal marked by the red oval frame, and the adjacent interference signal marked by the red frame. The detection result is shown in Fig. 6(b), where 1 indicates that the vehicle is detected and 0 indicates that the vehicle is not detected. ATA, SVA and DVA algorithms all result in false and missing detections of the vehicle signal. The MFDA algorithm eliminates both subway interference and adjacent interference, so it detects all vehicles correctly.

Table 2. Algorithm comparison

Algorithm	Actual number of vehicles	Number of correct detections	Detection Accuracy
ATA	1550	1163	75%
SVA	1550	1395	90%
DVA	1550	1426	92%
MFDA	1550	1520	98%

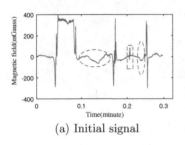

(a) Initial signal

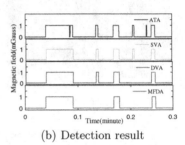

(b) Detection result

Fig. 6. Vehicle detection examples of three algorithms.

5 Conclusion

The magnetic sensor is easily affected by the magnetic interference produced by the urban subway system. This paper proposes an anti-interference algorithm for vehicle detection. We design two filters, the Gaussian structure morphological filter is used to extract the magnetic signal of the moving vehicle, and the rectangular structure morphological filter is used to extract the magnetic signal of the static vehicle. Experiment results show that the algorithm of vehicle detection has better detection accuracy than the traditional algorithms.

References

1. Cai, Z., Zheng, X., Yu, J.: A differential-private framework for urban traffic flows estimation via taxi companies. IEEE Trans. Ind. Inf. **15**(12), 6492–6499 (2019)
2. Bhaskar, L., Sahai, A., Sinha, D., Varshney, G., Jain, T.: Intelligent traffic light controller using inductive loops for vehicle detection. In: 2015 1st International Conference on Next Generation Computing Technologies (NGCT), pp. 518–522 (2015)
3. Chen, X., Kong, X., Xu, M., Sandrasegaran, K., Zheng, J.: Road vehicle detection and classification using magnetic field measurement. IEEE Access **7**, 52622–52633 (2019)
4. Dumberry, M., Finlayab, C.: Eastward and westward drift of the earth's magnetic field for the last three millennia. Earth Planet. Sci. Lett. **254**(2), 146–157 (2007)
5. Cheung, S., Varaiya, P.: Traffic surveillance by wireless sensor networks: final report. Technical report, California PATH, University of California, Berkeley, CA 94720 (2007)

6. Wang, Q., Zheng, J., Xu, H., Xu, B., Chen, R.: Roadside magnetic sensor system for vehicle detection in urban environments. IEEE Trans. Intell. Transp. Syst. **19**(5), 1365–1374 (2018)
7. Qiao, X., Zhao, Y.: Vehicle overload detection system based on magnetoresistance sensor. In: 2018 International Conference on Electronics Technology (ICET), Chengdu, pp. 102–105 (2018)
8. Yang, B., Lei, Y.: Vehicle detection and classification for low-speed congested traffic with anisotropic magnetoresistive sensor. IEEE Sens. J. **15**(2), 1132–1138 (2015)
9. Zhang, Z., He, X., Yuan, H.: An anti-interference traffic speed estimation system with wireless magnetic sensor networks. IEEE Trans. Ind. Inf. **16**(4), 2458–2468 (2020)
10. Lowes, F.J.: Dc railways and the magnetic fields they produce-the geomagnetic context. Earth Planets Space **61**(8), i–xv (2009)
11. Pirjola, R.: Modelling the magnetic field caused by a dc-electrified railway with linearly changing leakage currents. Earth Planets Space **63**(2), 991–998 (2011)
12. Padua, M.B., Padilha, A., Vitorello, I.: Disturbances on magnetotelluric data due to dc electrified railway: a case study from south easter brazil. Earth Planets Space **54**(8), 591–596 (2002)
13. Zhang, W., Wang, H., Teng, R., Xu, S.: Application of adaptive structure element for generalized morphological filtering in vibratio signal de-noising. In: 2010 3rd International Congress on Image and Signal Processing, vol. 7, pp. 3313–3317 (2010)
14. Dunkels, A., Gronvall, B., Voigt, T.: Contiki - a lightweight and flexible operating system for tiny networked sensors. In: IEEE International Conference on Local Computer Networks, pp. 455–462 (2004)
15. Dong, H., Wang, X., Zhang, C., He, R., Jia, L., Qin, Y.: Improved robust vehicle detection and identification based on single magnetic sensor. IEEE Access **6**, 5247–5255 (2018)

Estimation of Short-Term Online Taxi Travel Time Based on Neural Network

Liping Fu, Jianbo Li$^{(\boxtimes)}$, Zhiqiang Lv, Ying Li, and Qing Lin

Computer Science and Technology, Qingdao University Qingdao, Qingdao, CN 266071, China
flpqdu@163.com, lijianbo@188.com, lvzq7614@163.com

Abstract. Estimating the short-term online taxi travel time is an important content in urban planning and navigation forecasting systems. When estimating the taxi travel time, we need to take many factors, such as temporal correlation, spatial dependency, and external factors, into consideration. In this paper, we propose a model named DeepSTTE (Short-term Travel Time Estimation) to estimate the short-term online taxi travel time. Firstly, the model integrates external factors using the embedding method. Further, we leverage the classical convolution networks to obtain the spatial feature information of the original GPS trajectory, and use the temporal convolutional networks (TCN) to obtain the temporal characteristics. Finally, we estimate the online taxi travel time of the entire path by the auxiliary learning part. We perform lots of experiments with real datasets, showing that our model DeepSTTE reduces the errors and performs better than the current methods in estimating the travel time.

Keywords: Travel time estimation · Spatial feature · Temporal characteristic · TCN

1 Introduction

Online taxi rental has become a common phenomenon. When taking a taxi, people's primary concern must be the time spending on the road. Through the accurate estimation of the travel time of a taxi on the road, we arrange the best driving route. In the process of online car rental, we consider two types of time, waiting time and traveling time. The driver starts taking orders and passengers wait for the car in the waiting time. Traveling time is the time from the starting point when we take a taxi to the destination. So our research is to estimate the travel time of a taxi, which includes the traveling time and the waiting time. Through learning from historical data, we find that most of the trajectories

This research was supported in part by National Key Research and Development Plan Key Special Projects under Grant No. 2018YFB2100303, Shandong Province colleges and universities youth innovation technology plan innovation team project under Grant No. 2020KJN011 and Program for Innovative Postdoctoral Talents in Shandong Province under Grant No. 40618030001, National Natural Science Foundation of China under Grant No. 61802216, and Postdoctoral Science Foundation of China under Grant No. 2018M642613.

D. Yu et al. (Eds.): WASA 2020, LNCS 12385, pp. 20–29, 2020.
https://doi.org/10.1007/978-3-030-59019-2_3

were distributed within one hour and the distance was within 20 km. So we estimate the travel time of the online taxi in the short term.

Two main methods have been proposed to estimate the travel time. In the Individual methods, the travel time of each sub-path is estimated separately, and then added to obtain the time of the entire road. However, these methods ignore intersections and traffic lights, which are important to the estimation of travel time. In the Collective methods, the influences of intersections and traffic lights can be considered. But there exists data sparsity problem. This affects the accuracy of the estimated time and brings a negative influence to the estimate result.

Based on the consideration of several factors previously mentioned, we propose an end-to-end training-based model for Short-term Online Taxi Travel Time Estimation, called DeepSTTE. Our contributions can be summarized as follows:

- We introduce the external factors part and the spatio-temporal part. We use convolutional networks to obtain spatial dependency, and use Temporal Convolutional Networks (TCN) to capture temporal correlation.
- We design the auxiliary learning part, we estimate the travel time of the local path and the entire path simultaneously to get the optimal estimation result. And when estimating the entire path, we use the attention mechanism to give different weights according to the importance of different roads.
- We conduct a large number of experiments to evaluate our model by using taxi GPS trajectory data from Chengdu in August. The results show that the performance of our model is better than the state-of-the-art baselines.

2 Related Work

Road Segment-Based Travel Time: Lots of researches have done on loop detectors before GPS was used. Jia, Z et al. [1] presented a PeMS algorithm for travel time estimation by obtained vehicle speeds from loop detectors. Support vector machine (SVM) algorithm was used to estimate the speed of traffic flow in the road traffic network with high accuracy [2]. The accuracy rate of these methods was relatively low. These methods based on the every road segment to estimate the taxi travel time, the connection between the road and the other road was ignored. However in practical situations, we need to consider the connection between the roads. Besides, it was more difficult for us to obtain accurate travel time or speed of every road segment.

Path-Based Travel Time: Some methods used historical trajectory data to calculate the travel time of short-term online taxis. Luo, W et al. [3] used frequent path from historical trajectories to indicate the actual travel time of roads. Hull, B et al. [4] researched the dynamic travel time estimation that based on real-time travel time on probe vehicles. Rahmani, M et al. [5] proposed an efficient non-parametric method by using low-frequency floating car data (FCD) directly to estimate the given road travel time. Compared with road segment-based travel time method, these methods have better performance. However, there might also be data sparsity problems.

Deep Learning methods to estimate Travel Time: Deep learning methods play an important role in estimating road traffic. Wang, D et al. [6] proposed a model named DeepTTE. Long short-term memory was used to obtain the long-term time dependence of the time series. Zhang. H et al. [7] introduced a multi-feature extraction structure to improve the original single-interval loss, and proposed a dual-interval loss as a new auxiliary supervision model. Zhang. J et al. [8] built an end-to-end structure called ST-ResNet based on spatial-temporal data, for estimating the citywide crowd flows. These works show that deep learning has strong advantages in trajectory traffic estimation. In this paper, we firstly apply the CNNs and TCN as deep learning models to the road travel time estimation. In addition, we fully consider the spatial and temporal dependencies of the original GPS sequence.

3   Problem Definition

In this section, we introduce the short-term taxi travel time estimation problem. We define that a sequence of continuous historical GPS points as a historical driving trajectory Q, i.e., $Q = \{q_1, q_2, ..., q_n\}$. Each GPS point q_i *has* the latitude ($q_i.lat$), the longitude ($q_i.lon$) and the time stamp ($q_i.ts$). Besides, each trajectory is associated with the taxi ID (*driverID*), the day of the month (*dateID*), the day of the week (*weekID*), the passenger states of taxi (*states*), the beginning time of a trajectory(*timeID*).

In the driving trajectory, we propose other important attribute, the travel distance. We denote $dis(q_1, q_n)$ as the total distance of a travel path, i.e.,

$$dis(q_1, q_n) = \sum_{i=1}^{n-1} dis(q_i, q_{i+1}). \tag{1}$$

With the aforementioned definitions, the problem of short-term taxi travel time estimation is formulated as follows: set T be a driving trajectory on travel path. Given P as a query path, and P is contained in T. Our goal is to use the given historical paths to train models and learn model parameters which can estimate the travel time of the entire driving trajectory

4   Model Architecture

Firstly, we propose a model called DeepSTTE, as show in Fig. 1. DeepSTTE has three components: the spatio-temporal part, the external factors part and the auxiliary learning part. The model fully considers the temporal correlation and spatial dependency of the original GPS position sequence and the external information. The external factors part is used to deal with the external information of the trajectory. The Spatio-Temporal learning part aims at capturing the temporal and spatial dependencies of the road trajectory. Finally, we use the auxiliary learning part to achieve the balance of the local path time estimation and the entire path time estimation with learning the loss function.

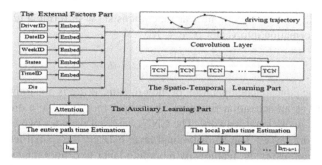

Fig. 1. DeepSTTE architecture

4.1 The External Factors Part

We present an external factors section to incorporate these external factors. Because these external factors are categorical, they can not be input directly into the neural network. We use the embedding method [9] to transform these categorical variables $l \in [L]$ into embedding space $R^{M \times 1}$. In this way, embedding can effectively reduce the dimensions and improve the training speed. Finally the embedded vector and the travel distance $dis(q_1, q_n)$ are concatenated as the output of the external factor, called *ext*.

4.2 The Spatio-Temporal Learning Part

We present the spatio-temporal learning part that consists of convolution networks layer and temporal convolutional networks layer.

Convolution Networks Layer

Firstly, we need to capture the spatial features of the raw GPS points. The previous works [10] propose to use graph embedding to capture the spatial information of the neighbourhood regions. In the paper [11], they only use nonlinear function to extract the spatial features. But we use a nonlinear function and convolutional neural networks (CNNs) to obtain spatial features [12], as show in Fig. 2. CNNs perform better in face recognition, speech recognition, natural language processing, and target tracking [12].

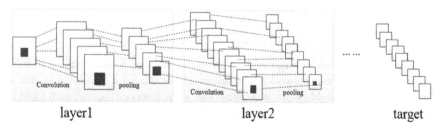

layer1   layer2   target

Fig. 2. Convolution layer

In the model, we first use a nonlinear function as show in formula (2) to map the path location information into vector $ploc_i \in 16$,

$$ploc_i = \tanh(W_{ploc} < q_{i.lat}, q_{i.lon} >) \tag{2}$$

$< >$ indicates the concatenate operation of the i-th path. W_{ploc} is a learning parameter matrix and Tanh is an activation function. The output $ploc$ is $16 \times n$ dimension and as input to the convolutional network. The CNNs we used includes two convolutional layers, two pooling layers. The convolutional layer extracts the spatial features of the path and then compresses the features by a pooling layer to extract the main features. (In the paper, we use max pooling). Using convolutional layer and pooling layer reduce the complexity of the parameters effectively, the model is greatly optimized. The output of the convolution layer is $conv^2$.

$$conv_i^1 = \sigma(W_{conv}^{(1)} \bullet ploc + b^{(1)}) \tag{3}$$

$$conv_i^2 = \sigma(W_{conv}^{(2)} \bullet conv_i^1 + b^{(2)}) \tag{4}$$

W_{conv}, b are the learnable parameters and σ is an activation function. Thus, we obtain the final feaure map, denoted as spa.

Temporal Convolutional Networks Layer
To further deal with the time correlation of local road segments, we use the time convolutional network (TCN). In TCN, the causal convolution and dilated convolution are used to deal with sequence problems [13]. The filter $F = (f_1, f_2, ..., f_K)$, the sequence $X = (x_1, x_2, ..., x_T)$, the causal convolution at x_t is:

$$(F * X)_{(x_t)} = \sum_{k=1}^{K} f_k x_{t-K+k} \tag{5}$$

Causal convolution has two significant characteristics. Firstly, we estimate y_t by the observed sequence without considering future information. Furthermore, the number of hidden layers increases with the amount of historical information. The dilated convolution with a dilatation rate d at x_t is:

$$(F *_d X)_{(x_t)} = \sum_{k=1}^{K} f_k x_t - (K - k)d \tag{6}$$

In practice, the dilatation rate increases with the number of network layers. (i.e., $d = O(2^n)$ at level n of the network). The advantage of dilated convolution is that it increases the receptive field, which guarantees that some filters can access each input in the effective history. So the output of each convolution contains a very large range of historical information.

The residual connection makes an element-wise connection to the input and output of the network by adding a shortcut connection. When the network is deep enough, the previous data information can skip one or more non-linear layers through the shortcut connection. This way greatly reduces the calculation amount of the network and does not generate additional parameters, but increases the training of the network speed and improves the training effect of the model.

In our model, the inputs of the temporal convolutional networks layer are the feature map *spa* and embedding vector *ext*, the updating states of the temporal convolutional networks layer are as follows.

$$r_i = \sigma(W_s \cdot spa + W_e \cdot ext + W_h \cdot r_{i-1}) \tag{7}$$

W_s, W_e, W_h are the learnable parameters and σ is an activation function. Finally, we obtain the spatio-temporal features sequence $\{r_1, r_2, r_3, \ldots, r_{|T|-k+1}\}$. Compared with LSTM (long short-term memory) [14] and GRU (gated recurrent unit) [15], TCN does not use gating mechanisms and it's structure is more concise and clear. When processing of the long time sequence, because of the filters shared across layers and the back propagation path that only depends on the depth of the network, TCN needs low memory for training

4.3 The Auxiliary Learning Part

We propose the auxiliary learning part as the third part of our model, which combines the obtained feature sequence and the related external information. We know that the local paths estimation ignores the impact of intersections and traffic lights and there exists data sparsity problem in the entire path estimation. In the auxiliary learning part, we estimate the local road segment and the entire path time simultaneously. In the local paths estimation segment, we use two fully connected layers to extract spatio-temporal features sequence $\{r_1, r_2, r_3, \ldots, r_{|T|-k+1}\}$ to a time sequence $\{h_1, h_2, h_3, \ldots, h_{|T|-k+1}\}$. Each h_i represents the estimated travel time of local paths $q_i \rightarrow q_{i+1} \rightarrow \cdots \rightarrow q_{i+k-1}$.

In the entire path estimation segment, we should pay more attention to the paths that contain traffic lights, intersections or other complex situations. The output of spatio-temporal learning part are input to the attention component to calculate the importance of different features based on specific paths, we obtain the vector r_{att}. The attention mechanism is currently widely used in different fields such as image processing, speech recognition, natural language processing etc. It will assign different probability information according to the importance of the result. Finally, we input r_{att} to the fully connected layers which are connected with residual connections. We get the estimated travel time of entire path, called h_{en}.

4.4 Model Training

We use an end-to-end approach to train our model. In the training phase, we estimate the travel time of all the local path and the entire path simultaneously. We define two loss functions. The former is defined as the average loss of all local paths.

$$L_l = \frac{1}{|T|-k+1} \sum_{i=1}^{|T|-k+1} \left| \frac{h_i - (q_{i+k-1} \cdot t_s - q_i \cdot t_s)}{q_{i+k-1} \cdot t_s - q_i \cdot t_s + \omega} \right| \tag{8}$$

The latter is defined as the correlation loss function of the entire path.

$$L_e = \left| h_{en} - (q_{|T|} \cdot t_s - q_1 \cdot t_s) \right| / (q_{|T|} \cdot t_s - q_1 \cdot t_s) \tag{9}$$

In the training phase, the loss function is defined as the weighted sum of L_l and L_e. Our target is to train the model to minimize the loss. α is a coefficient to balance the weights of L_l and L_e.

$$\text{loss} = \alpha \cdot L_l + (1 - \alpha) \cdot L_e \tag{10}$$

5 Experiments

In this part, we perform extensive experiments on the real trajectory dataset.

Datasets The datasats was generated by Chengdu Taxi in August 2014. The longest trajectory distance is 20 km. The shortest trajectory distance is 2 km. The maximum time of a trajectory is 3000 s. Each trajectory contains latitude and longitude with the external information(driverID, weekID, dataID, timeID.etc.).We set the data from the first three weeks as the training data and the data from the last week as the test data.

Parameter.
The External Factors Part: the embedding space of driverID, weekID, timeID is $R^{1 \times 16}$, $R^{1 \times 3}$, $R^{1 \times 8}$ respectively.

The Spatio-Temporal Part: In the CNNs, we set the number of the filters is 32, the kernel size is 3, the stride is 1, and choose RELU as the activation function. In the pooling layer, we choose maxpooling and set the kernel size and stride to 2.

The Auxiliary Learning Part: we set four residual fully-connected layers to estimate the entire path time, the dimension of each layer is 128.

We use Adam optimization algorithm [16] to train our model with 5-fold cross-validation for 200 epoches. The learning rate is 0.001 and the batch size is 64.

Evaluation Metric. We use three criterions including the mean absolute error (MAE), the rooted mean squared error (RMSE) and the mean absolute percentage error (MAPE) to evaluate our model.

Baseline Methods

HA: We select Tuesday(14:00 pm–16:00 pm) as the test data and estimate the travel time by the starting time and historical speed.
GBDT: Gradient Boosting Decision Tree is a widely used ensemble method to estimate the travel time [17]. In the model, GPS sequences of different lengths are sampled as equal-length sequences (128).
DeepTTE: DeepTTE is an end-to-end framework to estimate the travel time [6]. It uses CNN and LSTM to learn both the spatial and temporal correlations of the obtained GPS trajectories.

DeepTTE-RNN: The input of the model is same as DeepTTE. We use CNN and RNN to estimate the travel time.

Table 1 shows our experimental results. When we use historical average speed for estimation, the accuracy rate is low. GBDT has a significantly higher accuracy than HA, but it ignores the temporal dependency when processing data, resulting in a bad experimental result. Through experimental result, we find that the end-to-end method has a relatively high accuracy. DeepTTE and DeepTTE-RNN consider the spatial and temporal dependencies of data and the influence of external factors. And DeepTTE and DeepTTE-RNN use LSTM and RNN to extract time features respectively. The error rates are 11.26% and 12.37%. Finally, our model DeepSTTE has better performance with an error rate of 10.58%, which brings about 6%–14% decrease.

Table 1. Performance comparison of different methods

	MAE (sec)	RMSE (sec)	MAPE
HA	387.6757	582.5827	0.2813
GBDT	253.2008	356.3936	0.1925
DeepTTE-RNN	161.0623	272.1224	0.1237
DeepTTE	146.7305	252.3015	0.1126
DeepSTTE	138.8125	242.8759	0.1058

As we can see in Fig. 3.a, as the number of iterations increases, the RMSE of the three models decline steadily. Although there are occasional increases, the overall decline is obvious. Comparing with DeepTTE-RNN, the errors of our model DeepSTTE and DeepTTE decrease quickly, and the errors reduce significantly. Finally, we obtain a relatively lowest error.

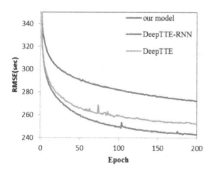
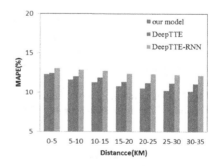

a. The error performance of different models   b. Comparison of MAPE and travel distance

Fig. 3. The performance of different models

As show in Fig. 3.b, we research the relationship between trajectory length and estimation accuracy, and compare DeepTTE and DeepTTE-RNN with our model Deep-STTE. As the distance of the trajectory increases, the MAPE of three models decreases. The result show when dealing with long paths, our model's MAPE is the smallest, so it has obvious advantages.

6   Conclusion

In this paper, we propose an end-to-end-based model to estimate the short-term online taxi travel time based on taxi historical trajectory data, which considers temporal correlations, spatial dependences and external factors containing holidays, weekends, driver's driving habits etc. We perform extensive experiments to evaluate the performance of DeepSTTE on the real trajectory dataset. Finally, we confirm our model has better performance in travel time estimation by comparing with the current methods.

References

1. Jia., Z., Chen, C., Coifman, B., Varaiya, P.: The PeMS algorithms for accurate, real-time estimates of g-factors and speeds from single-loop detectors. In: ITSC 2001, pp. 536–541. 2001 IEEE Intelligent Transportation Systems, Oakland (2001)
2. Asif, M.T., et al.: Spatio temporal patterns in large-scale traffic speed estimation. IEEE Trans. Intell. Transp. Syst. **15**(2), 794–804 (2014)
3. Luo, W., Tan, H., Chen, L., Ni, L.M.: Finding time period-based most frequent path in big trajectory data. In: Proceedings of ACM SIGMOD International Conference on Management of Data, pp. 713–724. Association for Computing Machinery, New York (2013)
4. Hull, B., et al.: CarTel: a distributed mobile sensor computing system. In: Proceedings of the 4th International Conference on Embedded Networked Sensor Systems, pp. 125–138 (2006)
5. Rahmani, M., Jenelius, E., Koutsopoulos, H.N.: Route travel time estimation using low-frequency floating car data. In: 16th International IEEE Conference on Intelligent Transportation Systems, pp. 2292–2297. The Hague (2013)
6. Wang, D., Zhang, J., Cao, W., Li, J., Zheng, Y.: When will you arrive? Estimating travel time based on deep neural networks. In: Thirty-Second AAAI Conference on Artificial Intelligence, pp. 2500–2507 (2018)
7. Zhang, H., Wu, H., Sun, W., Zheng, B.: DEEPTRAVEL: a neural network based travel time estimation model with auxiliary supervision. arXiv preprint arXiv:1802.02147 (2018)
8. Zhang, J., Zheng, Y., Qi, D.: Deep spatio-temporal residual networks for citywide crowd flows estimation. In: Thirty-First AAAI Conference on Artificial Intelligence, pp. 1655–1661 (2017)
9. Gal, Y., Ghahramani, Z.: A theoretically grounded application of dropout in recurrent neural networks. In: Advances in neural information processing systems, pp. 1019–1027 (2016)
10. Sun, Y., Jiang, G., Lam, S. K., Chen, S., He, P.: Bus travel speed estimation using attention network of heterogeneous correlation features. In: Proceedings of the 2019 SIAM International Conference on Data Mining, pp. 73–81. Society for Industrial and Applied Mathematics, Calgary (2019)
11. Qiu, J., Du, L., Zhang, D., Su, S., Tian, Z.: Nei-TTE: intelligent traffic time estimation based on fine-grained time derivation of road segments for smart city. IEEE Trans. Ind. Inform. **16**(4), 2659–2666 (2019)

12. Simonyan, K., Zisserman, A.: Very deep convolutional networks for large-scale image recognition. arXiv preprint arXiv:1409.1556 (2014)
13. Zhang, X., You, J.: A gated dilated causal convolution based encoder-decoder for network traffic forecasting. IEEE Access **8**, 6087–6097 (2020)
14. Hochreiter, S., Schmidhuber, J.: Long short-term memory. Neural Comput. **9**(8), 1735–1780 (1997)
15. Cho, K., Van Merriënboer, B., Bahdanau, D., Bengio, Y: On the properties of neural machine translation: encoder-decoder approaches. arXiv preprint arXiv:1409.1259 (2014)
16. Kingma, D.P., Ba, J.: Adam: a method for stochastic optimization. arXiv preprint arXiv:1412.6980 (2014)
17. Friedman, J., Hastie, T., Tibshirani, R.: The Elements of Statistical Learning. Springer Series in Statistics, vol. 1, no. 10. New York (2001)

Research on Algorithms for Finding Top-K Nodes in Campus Collaborative Learning Community Under Mobile Social Network

Guohui Qi[1,3,4], Peng Li[1,2,3(✉)], Hong Liu[1,3], Longjiang Guo[1,2,3], Lichen Zhang[1,2,3], Xiaoming Wang[1,2,3], and Xiaojun Wu[1,2,3]

[1] School of Computer Science, Shaanxi Normal University, Xi'an 710119, China
lipeng@snnu.edu.cn
[2] Key Laboratory of Modern Teaching Technology, Ministry of Education, Xi'an 710062, China
[3] Engineering Laboratory of Teaching Information Technology of Shaanxi Province, Xi'an 710119, China
[4] School of Graphic Information Center, Taiyuan Preschool Teachers College, Taiyuan 030400, China

Abstract. The continuous development and innovation of modern education theory and technology in the campus environment make the idea of "student-centered" become more and more popular. A variety of teaching forms with students as the dominant position appear. Computer-supported collaborative learning (CSCL) is now the primary form of collaborative learning. The current CSCL needs to be performed under the condition of network connection. Without a network, CSCL cannot be performed. The application of mobile social networks (MSN) will enable the dissemination of messages without network. Therefore, the efficiency of collaborative learning on campus will be greatly improved. This paper mainly studies the related algorithms of finding Top-k nodes in the campus community under the MSN environment to maximize the effect of collaborative learning. Finally, EpidemicRouter and SprayAndWaitRouter are experimental routes, analyzing the message delivery rate and response accuracy to verify the effectiveness of the algorithms.

Keywords: Collaborative learning · Campus · Influential · Top-k nodes · MSN

1 Introduction

Collaborative learning is a process of cooperation, interaction and common learning. In the collaborative learning scenario, students become the subject of knowledge production, which not only reduces the guidance pressure of teachers, but also helps strengthen team collaboration [1]. MSN refers to a network of opportunities given to social relationships determined by the carrier. There is no complete path between the source node and the destination node. Communication is achieved and optimized through the movement of nodes and social relationships between nodes [2]. In the campus collaborative learning community under MSN, finding Top-k nodes is essential for the fast and accurate

© Springer Nature Switzerland AG 2020
D. Yu et al. (Eds.): WASA 2020, LNCS 12385, pp. 30–38, 2020.
https://doi.org/10.1007/978-3-030-59019-2_4

propagation of messages. The campus environment is special, so it cannot be replaced by traditional Top-k algorithms.

2 Research Status

Finding Top-k nodes in social networks is equivalent to studying social influence. Li [3] made use of mobile crowdsourced data obtained from location-based social network services to study influence maximization in LBSNs. In social networks, the important nodes with great influence have a great influence on the structure and function of the network [4]. Jie Zhao [5] provides a quantitative model to measure the global importance of each node (GIN). How to mine the Top-k [6] nodes of the collaborative learning community is the basis for providing more favorable learning guidance for learner nodes. The authenticity [12] and privacy protection of information in social networks are also concerned.

There are many factors influencing campus collaborative learning. Social input was significantly positively correlated with group performance, while positive, negative, and confused three types of emotional input were negatively correlated with group performance [7]. Core self-evaluations and interpersonal familiarity have a positive influence on the identification with the group [8].

The calculation of the influence of nodes under Mobile Social Network (MSN) is different from the calculation of influence of nodes under Social Network Service (SNS) [9]. The messages in SNS can be fully transmitted. In MSN, nodes are opportunistic contacts.

3 Correlation Theory

3.1 Node Correlation

Node correlation, based on the number of hops between any two nodes and the weight of the edge to calculate the ratio of contact between two nodes. When any node contacts at least k nodes, each node will obtain node information with at least k hops. R_{dn} is the node correlation between node n and node d. r_{in} is the ratio that node d can reach node n via i-th hop node. l_i is the total number of contacts of i-th hop node, and l_{in} is the number of times that the i-th hop contacts the node n.

$$R_{dn} = r_{1n} + r_{2n} + r_{3n} + \cdots + r_{kn} \ (1 \leq i \leq k)$$

$$= \frac{l_{1n}}{l_1} + \sum_{i11}^{k11} \frac{l_{i11}}{l_1} \cdot \frac{l_{i11} \cdot l_{2n}}{l_{i11} \cdot l_2} + \sum_{i21}^{k21} \frac{l_{i21}}{l_1} \left(\sum_{i22}^{k22} \frac{l_{i21} \cdot l_{i22}}{l_{i21} \cdot l_2} \cdot \frac{l_{i21} \cdot l_{i22} \cdot l_{3n}}{l_{i21} \cdot l_{i22} \cdot l_{i3}} \right) \cdots \cdots$$

$$(1)$$

3.2 Node Accessibility

After the 120000 s-long time simulation experiment on infocome6 data set by One simulator, the statistics of 397 messages transmitted are as follows: The number of hops to complete the message transfer is mainly concentrated between 3–7 hops. When the source node is the same, the repeatability of the 1,2,3-th hop node is high. For 4-th and above hops, there is no obvious repetition. And the time complexity will increase as n increases in the calculation of R_{dn}. Therefore, the accessibility C_{dn} is defined as the 3-th hop and less than 3-th hop node correlation in the message transmission. Research is meaningful when two nodes are at least accessible. Defined as follows:

$$C_{dn} = r_{1n} + r_{2n} + r_{3n}$$
$$= \frac{l_{1n}}{l_1} + \sum_{i=1}^{f} \frac{l_{1i}}{l_1} \cdot \frac{l_{1i} \cdot l_{2n}}{l_{1i} \cdot l_2} + \sum_{j=1}^{a} \frac{l_{i21}}{l_1} \left(\sum_{k=1}^{g} \frac{l_{1j} \cdot l_{2k}}{l_{1j} \cdot l_2} \cdot \frac{l_{1j} \cdot l_{2k} \cdot l_{3n}}{l_{1j} \cdot l_{2k} \cdot l_3} \right) \tag{2}$$

The Learning Lead index L [10] is the reputation of the student node, and reflects the interaction between this node and other nodes in the collaborative learning process. The L can be defined as:

$$L_i = \varepsilon \cdot T_i \cdot \frac{T_i}{Q_i} \cdot \frac{H}{T_i - H_i} \cdot \frac{t_i}{H_i - t_i} = \frac{\varepsilon T_i^2 H_i t_i}{Q_i(T_i - H_i)(H_i - t_i)} \tag{3}$$

Where L_i is the Lead index of the node i. T_i is the number of the node i is asked. H_i is the number of replies from the node i. t_i is the number of acknowledged replies from the node i. Q_i is the number of questions from the node i. ε is a parameter for index L. LV_i reflects the number of questions and replies of node i, and the accuracy of replies. The definition of LV is as follows:

$$LV_i = \sum_{j=1}^{N-1} L_j R_{ij} \tag{4}$$

Where L_j is the learning Lead center of node j, R_{ij} is node i and node j accessibility, the total number of nodes n. The value is higher, the node in contact with the node L is higher.

3.3 Node Contact Centrality CV

In MSN's collaborative learning community, the degree of centrality of a node can be approximated as the node's ability to contact other nodes. The greater the number of nodes that a node can contact, the higher the centrality of the node. However, the quality of this node's contact with other nodes and the degree of the node's neighbors [11] should be considered. The definition of the contact centrality CV is defined as follows:

$$DE_j = \frac{d_j}{G - 1} \tag{5}$$

$$CV_i = \sum_{j=1}^{N-1} R_{ij} DE_j \tag{6}$$

The DE_j for node j centricity d_j for the number of the nodes in contact j. G is the total number of nodes. N is the number that node i can touch. R_{ij} is the contact between node i and node j. CV_i is the node contact centrality of node i.

4 Algorithm Design

4.1 General Update Algorithm(Ye)

The nodes are combined to find the overall Top-k without handling the transmission path. Ye is as follows: each node keeps the sequence $T(n, L_n)$, in which the number of nodes is not more than k; The nodes in the $T(n, L_n)$ sequence held by each node are sorted according to the L value. The advantage of this algorithm is that after continuous contact with other nodes, each node will maintain the more accurate Top-k node with the highest L_i value in the entire community, and the algorithm complexity is low. The disadvantage is that only the learning index L_i value is taken into consideration, that is, only the student's performance is outstanding, and the relationship between the nodes is not considered. If the found node has a weak social relationship with the node, it is not willing to be answer the question and the Top-k node loses meaning.

4.2 Update Algorithm Based on Accessibility(Tua)

The algorithm is based on the accessibility of nodes. Each node keeps three hop information, and each node selects its own Top-k node, instead of finding the whole Top-k node. Each node's own contact is updated by each contact. Each node maintains the quaternion information parameter $GUY(i, H_{ci}, C_i, L_i)$ for each node contacted. H_{ci} is the number of hops of the current node to the node, and C_i is the accessibility of the current node to the node. Finally, C_i is updated and all the nodes it keeps are sorted according to L value. The advantage of this algorithm is that it can fully transmit messages, that is to find its own Top-k node sequence. It not only considers the learning Lead index, whether the comprehensive performance of the student node is excellent, but also considers whether the excellent node is accessible to itself. However, its disadvantage is that it can not guarantee the quality of the received reply, that is, whether the contacted node is an active node, and whether it is willing to reply to messages.

4.3 Update Algorithm Based on Accessibility and Learning Centrality (Nla)

In the algorithm, each node selects a Top-k node according to the LV_i value. $GUY(i, H_{ci}, C_i, L_i, LV_i)$ for all nodes it has touched. Sequences T1 and T2 are arranged according to the values of L_i and LV_i. The message sent by each node is a message Mesg(resc, tar1, tar2) containing the secondary destination node, resc is the source node, tar1 is the first destination node, and tar2 is the second destination node.

The advantage of Nla algorithm is that it can transmit the message fully. Because it not only considers the learning Lead index, node contact, but also considers the learning centrality, the quality of the reply message can be greatly improved to a certain extent. The Top-k node sequence can not only reach the node with better comprehensive scores, but also consider whether the node is an active node. But time complexity and message delay increase. Nla only looks for its own to Top-k nodes, and does not consider the influence of the whole Top-k node sequence.

4.4 Evolutionary Algorithm(NC)

The nodes are combined to find the overall Top-k, and each node looks for adaptive propagation path. The basic idea of the Nc (see Fig. 1) is that each node maintains two node sequences $k1(n, L_n)$, $k2(m, H_{cm}, R_m, CV_m)$, and k1 is the Top-k node sequence of the L's value. When any two nodes meet, the L's values are exchanged for each other's L's values. If the L's value of the other is greater than $k1(n, L_n)$, the L's value of the last node in, the $k1(n, L_n)$ sequence is updated. The sequence of the other is updated according to the other's $k1(n, L_n)$ sequence. k2 is the node contact center order, considering that the contact between nodes is not reliable when the contact relationship is weaker than the "contactable node". So k2 only considers the contact intensity is greater than the "contactable node" node, only the three-hop node is considered. For the k2 sequence, when any two nodes come into contact, they exchange their H_c values of 1 and 2, add them to the node sequence they maintain. Then update H_c and R, and sort all nodes according to the CV values respectively.

```
The Nc algorithm is described as follows:
1: While node_i contact_with node_j do:
2:     Update K1i(n,Ln)
3:        If(j ⊆ k), Update K1i(n,Ln) with (node_j,Lnode_j)
4:        Else if(in<k),Add Ti(n,Ln) with (node_j,Lnode_j)
5:        Else if(Lnode_j>Ln_n)
6:           Delete (Ti_n,LTi_n) from Ti(n,Ln),and add (node_j,Lnode_j) to Ti(n,Ln);
7:        End if;
8:     Receive Tj(n,Ln) from node_j
9:        If (Tj-Ti∩Tj≠null)
10:          Update Ti(n,Ln) With Tj-Ti∩Tj
11:       End if
12:    Update k2(m,Hcm,Rm,CVm)
13:       Updae k2i(m,Hcm,Rm,CVm) With (j,Hcj,Rj,CVj);
14:       Receive k2j(m,Hcm,Rm,CVm) from node_j;
15:       If(jm>0),than Updae k2i(m,Hcm,Rm,CVm) With k2j(m,Hcm,Rm,CVm)
16:       While(0<k≤jm)
17:          If(mi∩k==null), add (k,Hck+1,Rjk·Rjk, CVk) to k2i(m,Hcm,Rm,CVm);
18:          End if;
19:          If(mi∩k≠null)
20:             If(Hcm-Hcm==2);
21:                update (k,Hck+1,Rjj+Rjj·Rjk, CVk) to k2i(m,Hcm,Rm,CVm)
22:             Else
23:             End if;
24:          End if;
25:       End While
26:    Sort_ k2i(m,Hcm,Rm,CVm)from large to small according to CVm;
27: end while
```

Fig. 1. The algorithm of Nc

When the node sends the question message, first check whether the k1 sequence node exists in the k2 sequence. If it exists, the question request can be sent directly, if not, the destination node is marked as the node of the k1 sequence. Setting the mediation destination node as the Top-k node of the k2 sequence, and send the mediation destination node.

5 Experiment

5.1 Description of the Experiment

The above algorithms are simulated using the MIT Reality data set as follows:

(1) In this paper, EpidemicRouter and SprayAndWaitRouter are selected as experimental routes for research. The random selection null method, Ye,Tua, Nla and Nc algorithm are used to calculate the message delivery rate and reply accuracy rate.

(2) Randomly set the reply message probability ε $(0 \leq \varepsilon \leq 1)$. The accuracy of reply to the message η $(0 \leq \eta \leq 1)$. When η. greater than or equal to 0.5, it is set as a Rep-T type message. Otherwise, it is a Rep-F type message.

(3) When the questioner node receives a Rep_T message, it counts as a successful reply. Otherwise, it counts as an Rep_F message. Finally, it counts the times of Q-type messages, Rep_T messages and Rep_F messages. $\sum Q$ is the total number of questions; $\left(\sum Rep\_T + Rep\_F\right)/\sum Q$ is the message delivery rate; $\sum Rep\_T/\sum Q$ is the probability of successfully reply; $\left(Rep\_T/\left(\sum Rep\_T + Rep\_F\right)\right)$ is the response accuracy of the reply message.

5.2 Experimental Results and Analysis

Because the choice of the routing algorithm and the value of k is different, it will affect the situation of Q, Rep_T, and Rep_F, so each algorithm needs to be statistics separately.

(1) When k = 4, the message delivery rate and response accuracy rate are as follows (see Fig. 2 and Fig. 3):

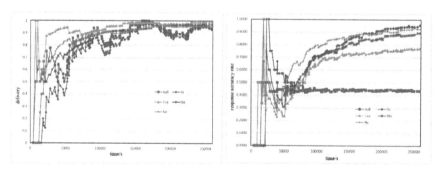

Fig. 2. The message delivery and response accuracy of the route is EpidemicRouter

As can be seen from Fig. 2, the delivery rate of each algorithm is similar. But the delivery rates of the algorithms null and Ye are slightly worse. Regarding the response accuracy rate, the algorithm Ye and Nc are high, which can reach more than 90% after stabilization. Nc algorithm is significantly better than other algorithms.

As can be seen from Fig. 3, the delivery rate of the algorithm Tua is the best and the algorithms Nla and Nc are similar. But the delivery rate of the algorithm Ye is poor.

The algorithms Ye and Nc have the highest response accuracy, but the algorithm Ye has large fluctuations. By analyzing the message delivery report, it can be seen that the main reason is that the algorithm Ye message delivery rate is low. Comprehensive analysis, algorithm Nc is superior to other algorithms.

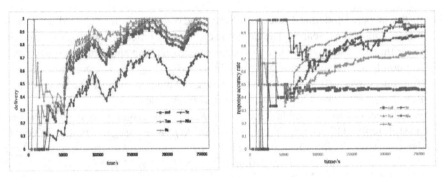

Fig. 3. The message delivery and response accuracy of the route is SprayAndWaitRouter

(2) When k = 10, the message delivery rate and response accuracy rate are as follows (see Fig. 4 and Fig. 5):

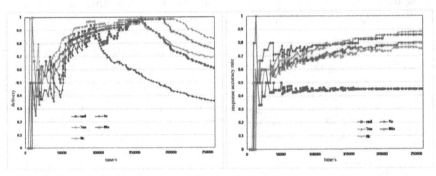

Fig. 4. The message delivery and response accuracy of the route is EpidemicRouter

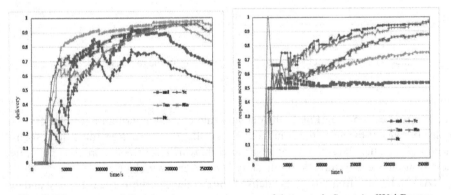

Fig. 5. The message delivery and response accuracy of the route is SprayAndWaitRouter

As can be seen from Fig. 4, the delivery rate of the algorithm Tua is the best, and the algorithm Ye is poor. According to the analysis of the message delivery report, it can be seen that there are many message passing nodes due to the large value of k, which causes some nodes to run out of energy. For message reply accuracy, the algorithms Ye and Nc are the highest, algorithm Nla is the second, and algorithm Tua is the worst. Comparing with Fig. 3, it can be seen that the response accuracy rates of the algorithms Ye, Tua, Nla, and Nc are all lower than those when k = 4. This is mainly because the value of k becomes larger, which results in more responses, resulting in uneven responses. However, comprehensive analysis, when k = 10, algorithm Nc is still better than other algorithms.

As can be seen from Fig. 5, the algorithm Tua has the best delivery rate and the slowest energy consumption, and the algorithm Ye performs the worst and has the fastest energy exhaustion. Aiming at the response accuracy rate, the algorithms Ye and Nc are relatively high and can reach over 95% after stabilization. Comprehensive analysis, algorithm Nc is slightly better than other algorithms.

5.3 Outlook

After analyzing the five algorithms, the algorithm Nc takes into account the Learning center LV and the node contact centrality CV. Finding Top-k nodes in the campus collaborative learning community, which is significantly better than other algorithms. The message delivery rate and response accuracy rate of the algorithm Nc are high and stable. However, the value of k has a greater impact on the message delivery rate of the algorithm Nc. Therefore, in the future work, we should conduct research on the value range of k under different conditions of nodes.

Acknowledgement. This work is partly supported by the National Natural Science Foundation of China under Grant No. 61877037, 61872228, 61977044; the National Key R&D Program of China under grant No. 2017YFB1402102: the Key R & D Program of Shaanxi Province under grant No. 2020GY-221, 2019ZDLSF07-01, 2020ZDLGY10-05; the Natural Science Basis Research Plan in Shaanxi Province of China under Grant No. 2020JM-303, 2020JM-302, 2017JM6060; the S&T Plan of Xi'an City of China under Grant No. 2019216914GXRC005CG006-GXYD5.1: the Fundamental Research Funds for the Central Universities of China under Grant No. GK201903090, GK201801004; the Shaanxi Normal University Foundational Education Course Research Center of Ministry of Education of China under Grant No. 2019-JCJY009.

References

1. Nasiri, E., Derakhshanfard, N.: FTR: features tree based routing in mobile social networks. Wireless Netw. **26**(1), 283–291 (2018). https://doi.org/10.1007/s11276-018-1809-x
2. Gomes, J.E.A.: Centrality-based group profiling: a comparative study in co-authorship networks. New Gener. Comput. **2017**(2), 1–31 (2017)
3. Li, J., Cai, Z., Yan, M., Li, Y.: Using crowdsourced data in location-based social networks to explore influence maximization. In: The 35th Annual IEEE International Conference on Computer Communications INFOCOM 2016
4. Liu, L.: Similarity measurement method based on node influence in heterogeneous networks. Chin. J. Electron. **47**(09), 1929–1936 (2019)

5. Zhao, J.: Identifying influential nodes in complex networks from global perspective. Chaos Solitons Fractals **133**(109637), 1–12 (2020)
6. Niu, B.: TOP-k query protocol for popular tag categories in large-scale dynamic RFID systems **42**(02), 36–51 (2019)
7. Yanyan, L.: Construction and application of analytical model of group learning input in online collaborative learning. China Distance Educ. **7**(02), 40–48 + 77 (2020)
8. Petru, L.: Identified and engaged: a multi-level dynamic model of identification with the group and performance in collaborative learning. Learn. Individ. Differ. **78**(101838), 1–9 (2020)
9. Hamid, S.: Understanding students' perceptions of the benefits of online social networking use for teaching and learning. Internet High. Educ. **26**, 1–9 (2015)
10. Jiang, S.: Domain integration entity link based on relation index and representation learning. Acta Autom. Sinica **2020**(1), 1–10 (2020). (Online publishing)
11. Ruan, M.: Centrality prediction based on K-order Markov chain in mobile social networks. Peer-to-Peer Netw. Appl. **12**(6), 1662–1672 (2019)
12. Lin, Y., Cai, Z., Wang, X., Hao, F.: Incentive mechanisms for crowdblocking rumors in mobile social networks. IEEE Trans. Veh. Technol. (TVT) **68**(9), 9220–9232 (2019)

VES: A Component Version Extracting System for Large-Scale IoT Firmwares

Xulun Hu[1,2], Weidong Zhang[1], Hong Li[1(✉)], Yan Hu[3], Zhaoteng Yan[1], Xiyue Wang[1], and Limin Sun[1]

[1] Institute of Information Engineering, Chinese Academy of Sciences, Beijing, China
lihong@iie.ac.cn
[2] School of Software and Microelectronics, Peking University, Beijing, China
[3] School of Computer and Communication Engineering,
University of Science and Technology Beijing, Beijing, China

Abstract. Open source components are widely used in IoT firmwares. Components of different versions have various vulnerabilities. For example, CVE-2020-8597 only affects specific version of pppd. Therefore, extracting the version of a component is of significance for discovering known vulnerabilities of devices. However, due to cross-architecture issue, extracting the versions of components from IoT firmwares in large scale is very challenging. To the best of our knowledge, there is no effective approach to extract component versions from large scale IoT firmwares. In this paper, we propose and implement an IR-based component Version Extracting and Recovering system for IoT firmwares, called VES. VES translates assembly codes into intermediate representation called VEX, and recovers the version string of a component by analyzing the dataflow of arguments of version-printing function. We implement VES and evaluate it on a large-scale dataset with 13,189 IoT firmwares of different architectures. VES can successfully extract the version information of 42,034 components with extraction rate of 96.48% and accuracy rate of 97.02%, which is 14.76% higher than the existing method.

Keywords: Firmware · Component · VEX IR

1 Introduction

A component is supplied as a SDK to provide a set of related functions for IoT firmwares. Recent years have witnessed a tremendous rise of IoT vulnerabilities, among which a large portion of vulnerabilities are caused by components of different version. For example, HeartBleed [4] only affects specific versions of *OpenSSL* [9]. However, when component vulnerabilities are exposed by security researchers, it is not clear which IoT firmware uses the corresponding version of components. Thus, identifying the versions of components in IoT firmwares are of great significance for vendors and national security departments to the discover newly released component vulnerabilities.

© Springer Nature Switzerland AG 2020
D. Yu et al. (Eds.): WASA 2020, LNCS 12385, pp. 39–48, 2020.
https://doi.org/10.1007/978-3-030-59019-2_5

Currently, there are two main approaches to get versions of components in IoT firmwares. One approach is to run the component and use commands, such as "–version". However, this approach requires simulation environment or real devices, and there are a large number of IoT devices with various architectures. Therefore, it's not conducive for analysis in large-scale. Another approach is to remotely interact with IoT devices. For example, Sarabi *et al.* [10] extract the component name and version information by obtaining the banner information of online devices. However, this method cannot get version of a component without open network interfaces.

It is very challenging to design and implement a scalable component version extracting method for large-scale IoT firmwares. Firstly, IoT firmwares use different architectures [5] such as *MIPS*, *ARM* and *X86*, and thus they have different ISA (Instruction Set Architecture). The syntax rules are inconsistent for binaries of different schemas. Secondly, traditional analysis methods and tools in the component analysis of firmware, to a certain extent, rely on manual filtering, *i.e.* needing to manually judge the component version information, so it is difficult to achieve automatic large-scale component version extraction. Thirdly, there is no publicly available ground truth dataset to evaluate the performance of the proposed method.

In this paper, we design and implement a component Version Extracting System for large-scale IoT firmwares, termed as VES. VES converts component binaries of different architectures into intermediate representations of the same syntax rules, and then statically extract version information of components by analyzing the parameter data of the printed version codes in the components through data flow. Since there is no publicly available component version information data set, we collect 251 firmwares with different architectures and manually mark 2,921 component version information. We compare VES with simulating running and network extraction method [10]. The results show that VES can extract the version of a component within 0.7 s in average, and the accuracy rate is 97.02% which is 14.76% higher than the existing method. We also test VES on a large-scale dataset with 13,189 IoT firmwares. VES successfully identifies the versions of 42,034 components, and the extraction rate is 96.48%. The main contributions of this paper are summarized as follows:

- In this paper, we design and implement a component version extracting system for large-scale cross-architecture IoT firmwares.
- We build a ground truth dataset containing 251 firmwares with different architectures and 2,921 components with version information. The dataset will be publicly available for other researchers.
- We extensively evaluate VES both on the ground truth dataset and a large-scale dataset with 13,189 IoT firmwares. The experimental results show VES can extract the version of a component within 0.7 s in average, with accuracy rate of 97.02%, which is 14.76% higher than the existing method. VEX can identify the versions of 42,034 components from 13,189 IoT firmwares with extraction rate of 96.48%.

2 Background and Preliminary Knowledge

2.1 Version Strings in Components

The version information of the component is stored in component binary file in the form of strings. When component runs, it will call printing function to print out the version string of the component. Version stored in component file have two forms: one is integrated string (eg. BusyBox v1.22.1) and the other is formatted (eg. pppd version %s). The integrated string can be filtered out from component file by regex. However, the formatted version string (fvs) and the version number string (vns) are stored in different data addresses in the component file. When the component calls the printing function, the printing function's arguments are passed into argument registers or stacks, and the integrated version string is printed out by replacing the placeholder of fvs by vns. For example, in the source code of component *pppd*, the code that prints version information is 'fprintf (stderr, "pppd version %s\n", VERSION)'. If the component is *ARM* arch, when it calls the function, "pppd version %s\n" and "VERSION" will be passed into *r1* and *r2* registers respectively. So we can extract the version of component by analyzing the parameters of the component's printing version function. Therefore, the static version extraction problem can be transformed into a function parameter extraction problem in a binary file.

2.2 Function Calling Convention

Function calling convention describes the rules of passing arguments into a subroutine. And different architectures have various calling conventions [7]. For *X86* architecture, when a function is called, the stack pointer points to the bottom of the stored parameter area, and then the function's arguments are pushed into the stack in right-to-left order. *ARM* and *MIPS* have their own arguments register. *ARM* uses *r0–r4* register to pass the first to fourth arguments of the calling function, and first four arguments are passed into *a0–a3* in *MIPS*. If the number of arguments of *ARM* or *MIPS* calling function is greater than four, the extra arguments are passed to the stack in order.

2.3 Intermediate Representation

Intermediate representation is a kind of abstracted representation which can abstract different codes to same representation. The VEX IR [8] can translate different ISAs assembly codes into the same representation.

3 Framework and Algorithm

3.1 Method Overview

In this paper, we propose a IR-based Version Extracting System, called VES, which can solve the large-scale cross-architecture formatted version extraction problem of IoT components. The framework of VES is shown in Fig. 1. For a component binary, VES deals with it by two steps. First, VES pre-processes the component binary, including accessing the formatted version string pattern ($fvsp$) from Component Formatted Version Pattern Database ($CFV\ PDB$), which is pre-created. And VES uses $fvsp$ to filter the component's strings. Then VES uses Formatted Version strings detector to find the Data Reference address ($DREF$) of the formatted version string from component binary. Meanwhile, the component binary is converted into VEX IR in *Vex IR translator*. Second, VES extracts the basic block of $DREF$. And VES analyzes the VEX IR statements to simulate the local stack space. And then by analyzing the data-flow of $fvsp$ variable in the VEX IR statements, VES finds the final position where the variable passed as the parameter of printing function. After that, VES calculates the position of vns by the position of fvs and the placeholder offset which represents vns in the formatted version string. Finally, by tracing backward the data-flow of the position of vns, VES finds the address of vns and gets vns from data segments of the component binary.

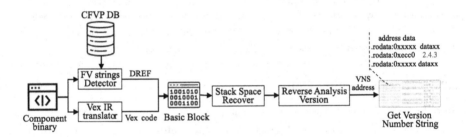

Fig. 1. The framework of VES

3.2   Pre-processing

Creating Component Formatted Version Patterns Database. In order to filter fvs from the component binary strings in large scale, we select the components with formatted version string as the components for large-scale analysis, and the corresponding formatted version string template is stored into patterns database. Specifically, as Fig. 2 shows, we crawl online sources for integrated version strings of open source components and we use regex to replace the version number in the integrated version string by placeholder '%s'. And we collect 126 various type of components whose version information are formatted forms. And we store them and its formatted version string patterns into patterns database for large-scale analysis.

Formatted Version Strings Detection. This module is utilized to filter out fvs in component binary file.

VEX IR Translator. Translating the assembly codes to VEX IR and extracting the basic block which refers the data of formatted version string. By this step, different ISAs are converted to the same intermediate representations.

Fig. 2. Creating patterns database process

3.3 Data-Flow of Arguments

After getting the VEX IR statements, VES analyzes the statements and extracts vns. Before that, we put forward some definitions about data-flow:

The semantic of a statement constrains the data-flow of the statement. The data-flow before and after a statement s are marked as $IN[s]$ and $OUT[s]$ respectively. The relationship between the data-flow before and after an assignment statement is called transfer function. If information propagates forward along the executing statements, transfer function of the statement could be recorded as f_s. The transfer function takes the data-flow of previous statement as input and produces a new data-flow after the statement, which represents as $OUT[s] = f_s(IN[s])$. In the condition of analyzing the backward-flow, the transfer function f_s of a statement converts a data-flow value after the statement to a new data-flow value before the statement, which represents as $IN[s] = f_s(OUT[s])$.

In the process of version arguments extraction, VES firstly finds the location of fvs. Algorithm 1 presents this step. For each statement in VES basic block, if its $IN[S]$ loads fvs address (add_{fvs}) to memory, VES traces the forward data-flow of $OUT[s]$ to find where it is passed as argument. If the traced statement's $OUT[s]$ presents a argument location, and the statement's $IN[s]$ is in the data-flow set of add_{fvs}, and its $OUT[s]$ is the location add_{fvs} passed.

3.4 Version Arguments Extraction

After getting add_{fvs}, as the Fig. 3 shows, VES calculates loc_{vns}, the location of vns. For *ARM* or *MIPS* architecture, the first four argument are stored in argument register. The loc_{vns} can be calculated by adding loc_{fvs} with the offset of placeholder in fvs which represents vns. For example, if the loc_{fvs} is *r1* and fvs is 'pppd version %s\n', the first placeholder in fvs represents vns, so vns is passed next to fvs, the location of vns is *r2*.

Algorithm 1: analysis the location of fvs

Input: add_{fvs}, Basic Block S_{BB}, $L \leftarrow IN[s]$ of add_{fvs}'s statement
Output: the location of fvs: loc_{fvs}

1 **for** s in S_{BB} **do**
2   **if** $IN[s]$ in L **then**
3   **if** *GetValueOf*($OUT[s]$) *is arg location* **then**
4   loc_{fvs} =**GetValueOf**($OUT[s]$);
5   **Return** loc_{fvs};
6   **else if** *GetValueOf*($OUT[s]$) *is temporary variable* **then**
7   L.**append**(**GetValueOf**($OUT[s]$));

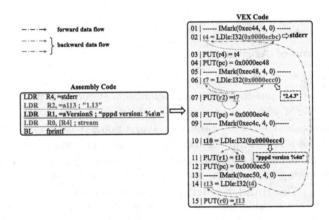

Fig. 3. The process of data flow analysis for extracting version information

3.5 Stack Space Recover

For *X86* architecture or the function with more than four arguments, arguments are passed by stack. In this case, arguments cannot be obtained directly by tracing the data-flow of the parameter register. To solve the problem, VES simulates recovering the stack space of the basic block.

More specifically, we propose Algorithm 2 to analyze the operations of modifying stack pointer and pushing operation. For VEX IR Basic Block, VES gets the temporary variable which represents SP pointer v_{sp} and stores the variable as the stack base. And for every statements of the basic block, VES analyzes the functionality of the statement. If the statement modifies the SP pointer, VES pushes the temporary variable of the $OUT[s]$ of statement to the stack which VES simulates. And then, VES tracks data flow of the temporary variables which represent the address of stack addresses. By this step VES gets the assignment statement of these temporary variables, and VES analyzes the data flow of the assignment expression to get the definition of the expression. Finally, the value of the definition is the value stored at the corresponding stack address. After getting the stack arguments, VES analyzes the location of the stack variables, combining placeholder in formatted version string to get vns data address.

Algorithm 2: recover stack space

Input: Basic Block S_{BB}, Set of SP related varibles $L \leftarrow v_{sp}$
Output: Set of stack pointer variables and stack address offset: $S \leftarrow \emptyset$

1 **for** *statement s in S_{BB}* **do**
2   **if** *$IN[s]$ is **modify** variable in L* **then**
3      $SP_{offset} = $ **Calculate**$(IN[s], S)$;
4   L.**append(VariableOf(**$OUT[s]$**))**;
5   S.**append(VariableOf(**$OUT[s]$**)** $: SP_{offset}$**)**;
6      $s_{assign} = $ **TraceForward(VariableOf(**$OUT[s]$**))**;
7   **if** ***GetValueOf***$(IN[s_{assign}])$ *is constant value* **then**
8        $value_{sp} = $ **GetValueOf**$(IN[s_a ssign])$;
9   **else if** ***ValueOf***$(IN[s_{assign}])$ *is temporary variable* **then**
10        $value_{sp} = $ **TracebackValue(GetValueOf(**$IN[s_{assign}]$**))**;

---

4 Evaluation

4.1 Dataset

Ground Truth. Since there is no binary data sets of IoT components with labeled version information in different architectures. We collect 251 different architectural firmwares and extract 2,921 components. And we label the version of the components manually.

Real World Dataset. To test the performance of VES in large-scale, we crawl 13,189 firmwares with different architectures from different IoT vendor websites (eg. dlink [1]). Through decompression, we screen out 43,556 of them with formatting version string, and the components are used to test VES's component version analysis capability in large-scale.

4.2 Accuracy and Efficiency

In first experiment, we use VES in the ground truth dataset and compare VES with other two methods. One method is to run the component dynamically by qemu [2], and get the versions by command line. Another method is to obtain the version by the network interface of running component in simulation [10]. The results are shown in Table 1. Among the 2,921 components tested, VES extracts 2,834 components versions with an accuracy of 97.02% and the average analysis time of most components is about 0.7 s. While 2,414 components versions are extracted by command-line method, the accuracy is 82.26%. However, we only get 39 versions of components by the network interface of running component in simulation. Because the other two methods need simulate environment and rely on manual work, VES saves the time and has a higher time efficiency.

Table 1. Result of the version extraction.

Arch	VES (acc)	qemu (acc)	Network (acc)	Total
MIPS	2219(98.05%)	1817(80.29%)	11(0.48%)	2263
ARM	506(90.11%)	483(90.11%)	24(4.47%)	536
X86	109(89.34%)	114(93.4%)	4(3.27%)	122
Total	2834(97.02%)	2414(82.26%)	39(1.3%)	2921

4.3   Implement in Real-World

In this experiment, we use our method for large-scale component version extraction. The versions of 43,566 components is successfully identified from 13,189 firmwares which contains 43,566 components in total. The extraction rate is 96.48%. The extraction results of the versions of the five most used components are shown in Table 2, so our method is also highly effective in large-scale analysis.

Table 2. Result of version extraction in large-scale

Component	Version extract (number)	VES num	Total
pppd	2.4.7(4367) 2.4.6(6) 2.4.5(2109) 2.4.4(3258) 2.4.3(398) 2.4.2b3(66) 2.4.2b1(13) 2.4.2(50) 2.4.1(61)	10328	10416
iptables	1.4.10(623) 1.4.6(649) 1.4.5(3) 1.4.4(54) 1.4.2(13) 1.4.0rc1(7)1.4.0(382) 1.3.8(1466) 1.3.5(50) 1.3.3(55) 1.2.9(3) 1.2.8(2) 1.2.7a(74) 1.2.6a(7) 0.9(15)	6133	6149
xtables-multi	1.4.21(4377) 1.4.17(1) 1.4.16.3(13) 1.4.12.2(15) 1.4.12.1(153) 1.4.12(8)	4467	4467
snmpd	5.7.2(8) 5.4.1(33) 5.0.9(2264) 4.1.2(2)	2307	2359
radvd	2.10(1) 1.13(124) 1.10.0(3) 1.9.8(2) 1.9.7(2) 1.9.3(7) 1.9.1(391) 1.8.5(3) 1.8.3(53) 1.8.1(118) 1.7(198) 1.6(4) 1.5(287) 1.4(1) 1.2(569) 1.13(124) 1.1(3) 1.0(19) 0.91(5)	1858	1877

5 Related Work

For the cross-architecture problem of binary files, Gemini [11] and Gao [6] classified the instructions of different architectures, used structural and instruction features to convert binary code functions into embedding vectors for similarity comparison. Valgrind [8] proposed VEX IR, and Asm2Vec [3] convert binary files under different architectures to VEX IR, and generates different signatures for detecting binary code similarity.

6 Conclusion

In this paper, we design and implement a component version extracting system for large-scale IoT firmwares. We evaluate our method by two experiments. The experiments show that 97.02% of the components in our dataset can be extracted version in about 0.7 s. In real-world large-scale experiment, our method can extract 96.48% components' version from 43,566 samples.

Acknowledgements. This work is supported by the National Key R&D Program of China (Grant No.2018YFB0803402), the National Natural Science Foundation of China (Grant 61702503, Grant U1766215 and Grant 61802016, the Interdisciplinary Research Project for Young Teachers of USTB (Fundamental Research Funds for the Central Universities) under Grant FRF-IDRY-19-016, the National Social Science Foundation of China under Grant 17ZDA331.

References

1. dlink firmwares website. http://files.dlink.com.au/Products/
2. Bellard, F.: QEMU, a fast and portable dynamic translator. In: 2005 Proceedings of the Annual Conference on USENIX Annual Technical Conference (2005)
3. Ding, S.H.H., Fung, B.C.M., Charland, P.: Asm2Vec: boosting static representation robustness for binary clone search against code obfuscation and compiler optimization. In: 2019 IEEE Symposium on Security and Privacy (SP) (2019)
4. Durumeric, Z., et al.: The matter of heartbleed. In: Proceedings of the 2014 Conference on Internet Measurement Conference, pp. 475–488 (2014)
5. Feng, Q., Zhou, R., Xu, C., Cheng, Y., Testa, B., Yin, H.: Scalable graph-based bug search for firmware images. In: Proceedings of the 2016 ACM SIGSAC Conference on Computer and Communications Security, pp. 480–491 (2016)
6. Gao, J., Yang, X., Fu, Y., Jiang, Y., Sun, J.: VulSeeker: a semantic learning based vulnerability. In: Proceedings of the 33rd ACM/IEEE International Conference on Automated Software Engineering - ASE 2018, Montpellier, France, 03–09 September 2018. ACM Press (2018)
7. Hu, Y., Zhang, Y., Li, J., Gu, D.: Binary code clone detection across architectures and compiling configurations. In: 2017 IEEE/ACM 25th International Conference on Program Comprehension (ICPC), pp. 88–98. IEEE (2017)
8. Nethercote, N., Seward, J.: Valgrind: a framework for heavyweight dynamic binary instrumentation. ACM Sigplan Not. **42**(6), 89–100 (2007)

9. Heartbleed OpenSSL bug CVE-2014-0160. http://cve.mitre.org/cgi-bin/cvename. cgi?name=CVE-2014-0160
10. Sarabi, A., Liu, M.: Characterizing the internet host population using deep learning: a universal and lightweight numerical embedding. In: 2018 Proceedings of the Internet Measurement Conference, pp. 133–146 (2018)
11. Xu, X., Liu, C., Feng, Q., Yin, H., Song, L., Song, D.: Neural network-based graph embedding for cross-platform binary code similarity detection. CoRR abs/1708.06525 (2017). http://arxiv.org/abs/1708.06525

Virtual Location Generation for Location Privacy Protection in VANET

Zhihong Li[1,2], Xiaoshuang Xing[1(✉)], Gaofei Sun[1(✉)], Zhenjiang Qian[1], and Jin Qian[3]

[1] School of Computer Science and Engineering, Changshu Institute of Technology, Suzhou, China
20195227095@stu.suda.edu.cn, {xing,gfsun,qianzj}@cslg.edu.cn
[2] School of Computer Science and Technology, Soochow University, Suzhou, China
[3] School of Computer Science and Technology, Taizhou University, Taizhou, China
qianjin@tzu.edu.cn

Abstract. Thanks to the wide development of the vehicular ad-hoc network (VANET), users can enjoy diverse location-based services (LBSs) on route. However, these LBSs also bring location privacy issues, which seriously threaten the personal privacy of VANET users. This paper aims at protecting the location privacy of VANET users by proposing a virtual location generation scheme. A VANET user reports a virtual location generated by our scheme instead of its actual location to the LBS server. The quality of service (Qos) loss metric and the location privacy metric are designed to evaluate the performance of the proposed scheme in a quantitative way. Numerical analysis is conducted and the impacts of different parameters on the performance of the scheme are analyzed.

Keywords: Vehicular Ad-hoc Network (VANET) · Location-based service (LBS) · Location privacy · Virtual location generation

1 Introduction

Vehicular Ad-Hoc Network (VANET) has become an active area of research, standardization, and development because it has tremendous potential to improve road safety, traffic efficiency, and driving comfort [17]. Typical VANET applications include assisted driving, road traffic information query, intelligent navigation, and so on [8,19], most of which are location-based services (LBSs). While enjoying the great benefits brought by these LBSs, intrusted LBS servers can reveal users' sensitive information such as personal interests and life styles based on the user's disclosed locations and query attributes, which seriously threatens the privacy of users [1,2,5,6].

Various location privacy protection schemes including k-anonymity based schemes and pseudonyms based schemes have been proposed in literature [13,20]. Traditional k-anonymity based schemes assume the existence of a trusted third party (TTP) [11] which hides a user's location in a cloaking region containing

© Springer Nature Switzerland AG 2020
D. Yu et al. (Eds.): WASA 2020, LNCS 12385, pp. 49–58, 2020.
https://doi.org/10.1007/978-3-030-59019-2_6

$k-1$ other users. Zhang et al. pointed out in [18] that once the TTP is attacked, it will completely expose the user's location. To deal with this challenge, distributed k-anonymity based schemes are proposed where k neighbouring users form a cloaking region in a distributed way independent of the TTP [3,4]. However, these distributed schemes can not be implemented in low traffic density scenarios since the requirement of at least k neighboring users can not be satisfied. Pseudonyms based schemes mainly investigate the time, location, and frequency for pseudonyms change. [14] pointed out that attackers can still effectively track the vehicles when users change their pseudonyms independently. To alleviate this problem, mix-zone schemes were proposed which require all vehicles to change their pseudonyms at predefined mix-zones [10,12]. However, the performance of these schemes are highly dependent on the information entropy of the mix-zones. Therefore, mix-zone schemes can also not be implemented effectively in low traffic density scenarios.

Virtual location based schemes are effective for location privacy protection when the traffic density requirements of the aforementioned schemes can not be satisfied. In [7], a user uses Hilbert curves to transform its location and sends the transformed location to the LBS server. [16] generates dummies through random pattern and rotation pattern to preserve users' location privacy. However, these schemes do not consider the moving direction of the users when generating the virtual locations. Therefore, they are not suitable for VANET applications. Besides, reporting the virtual location to the LBS server will lead to a quality of service (Qos) loss compared with reporting the actual location. It is challenging to quantitatively measure the Qos loss and the location privacy, and propose a virtual location generation scheme that balances the Qos loss and the location privacy for VANET users. This paper deals with these challenges and the contributions are summarized as follows:

1. We propose a virtual location generation scheme where a user generates its virtual location based on its own moving direction and Qos requirement independent of neighboring vehicles and trusted TTPs.
2. Two metrics are designed to quantitatively measure the Qos loss and the location privacy.
3. Numerical analyses are conducted to reveal the affects of different parameters on the performance of the proposed scheme in terms of the Qos loss and the location privacy

The rest of the paper is organized as following. In Sect. 2, we describe the problem to be solved and design the virtual location generation scheme. Section 3 analyzes the attack model of adversaries. The Qos loss metric and the location privacy metric are designed in Sect. 4. Section 5 investigates the proposed scheme through numerical analysis and we conclude the paper in Sect. 6.

2   Problem Description and Virtual Location Generation

2.1   Problem Description

Assume that there is a VANET user who reports its location and the service request to the LBS server in a driving vehicle. With the existence of adversaries, such as an intrusted LBS server or malicious users who can access to the LBS database, there is a risk of location privacy breaches if the VANET user's actual location is sent to the LBS server [9]. Therefore, the VANET user is motivated to report a virtual location for privacy protection. In this case, the user will experience a loss of the Qos since the service is provided according to the virtual location. It is necessary to design a virtual location generation scheme that protects the location privacy of the user while maintaining a low Qos loss.

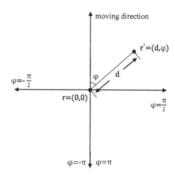

Fig. 1. Illustration of the polar coordinate system

Formulate a polar coordinate system with the actual location of the user being the reference point and the moving direction of the user being the reference direction. Let $r = (0,0)$ denote the actual location and $r' = (d, \varphi)$ denote the virtual location. Here, d is the distance from $r = (0,0)$ and φ is the angle from user's moving direction as shown in Fig. 1. We will design probability distribution functions (PDFs) for d and φ such that the VANET user can protect its location privacy by generating a virtual location according to the PDFs. To maintain a low Qos loss, the PDFs should be designed such that the virtual location with small d and φ is generated with high probability.

2.2   PDF of d

Intuitively, the Qos loss increases with d. When the Qos loss reaches a threshold, the service provided by the LBS server will not be able to satisfy the VANET user's Qos requirement. Therefore, we set an upper bound d_{max} for the value of d. In other words, d takes value from 0 to d_{max}, i.e. $d \in [0, d_{max}]$. Divide the interval $[0, d_{max}]$ into m subintervals with sub-interval SI_j, $j = 1, 2, \cdots, m$, being $[\frac{(j-1)d_{max}}{m}, \frac{jd_{max}}{m}]$. Take the mean values of the m subintervals as the value range of d, we get $d \in \{\frac{d_{max}}{2m}, \frac{3d_{max}}{2m}, \cdots, \frac{(2m-1)d_{max}}{2m}\}$. When $m \to +\infty$, d takes value continuously from $[0, d_{max}]$.

To make sure that d takes small values with high probabilities, we let d follow truncated exponential distribution on $[0, d_{max}]$. According to [15], the probability density function of d can be given as

$$f(d) = \begin{cases} \frac{\lambda_d e^{-\lambda_d d}}{1 - e^{-\lambda_d d_{max}}}, & d \in [0, d_{max}] \\ 0, & else \end{cases} \qquad (1)$$

Here, λ_d is the parameter of the exponential distribution. Then, the probability that d takes a specific value $d_j = \frac{(2j-1)d_{max}}{2m}$, $j = 1, 2, \cdots, m$, is calculated by integrating $f(d)$ from $\frac{(j-1)d_{max}}{m}$ to $\frac{jd_{max}}{m}$. Therefore, the PDF of d can be given as

$$Pr(d = d_j) = \frac{e^{-\lambda_d \frac{(j-1)d_{max}}{m}} - e^{-\lambda_d \frac{jd_{max}}{m}}}{1 - e^{-\lambda_d d_{max}}}, \qquad j = 1, 2, \cdots, m \qquad (2)$$

2.3   PDF of φ

Let φ take value from $[-\pi, \pi]$. As shown in Fig. 1, $\varphi = 0$ indicates the moving direction of the VANET user and $\varphi = \pi$ (or $\varphi = -\pi$) indicates the opposite direction of the moving direction. φ increases from 0 to π on the right-hand side of the moving direction (referred to as the right-hand side in short) and decreases from 0 to $-\pi$ on the left-hand side of the moving direction (referred to as the left-hand side in short). We assume that the virtual location is generated on the right-hand side and on the left-hand side with equal probability. Therefore, $Pr(\varphi \in [0, \pi]) = Pr(\varphi \in [-\pi, 0]) = \frac{1}{2}$. In the following, we will derive the PDF of φ on the right-hand side. Then, the PDF of φ on the left-hand side can be obtained readily.

Divide the interval $[0, \pi]$ into n subintervals with subinterval SI_i, $i = 1, 2, \cdots, n$, being $[\frac{(i-1)\pi}{n}, \frac{i\pi}{n}]$. Take the mean values of the n subintervals as the value range of φ on the right-hand side, we get $\varphi \in \{\frac{\pi}{2n}, \frac{3\pi}{2n}, \cdots, \frac{(2n-1)\pi}{2n}\}$. When $n \to +\infty$, φ takes value continuously from $[0, \pi]$. In order to make sure that φ takes angles close to the VANET user's moving direction with high probabilities, we let φ follow truncated exponential distribution on $[0, \pi]$. The probability density function of φ on the right-hand side can be given as

$$f_{right}(\varphi) = \begin{cases} \frac{1}{2} \cdot \frac{\lambda_\varphi e^{-\lambda_\varphi \varphi}}{1 - e^{-\lambda_\varphi \pi}}, & \varphi \in [0, \pi] \\ 0, & else \end{cases} \qquad (3)$$

Here, λ_φ is the parameter of the exponential distribution. Then, the probability that φ takes a specific value $\varphi_i = \frac{(2i-1)\pi}{2n}$, $i = 1, 2, \cdots, n$, is calculated by integrating $f(\varphi)$ from $\frac{(i-1)\pi}{n}$ to $\frac{i\pi}{n}$. Therefore, the PDF of φ on the right-hand side can be given as

$$Pr_{right}(\varphi = \varphi_i) = \frac{1}{2} \cdot \frac{e^{-\lambda_\varphi \frac{(i-1)\pi}{n}} - e^{-\lambda_\varphi \frac{i\pi}{n}}}{1 - e^{-\lambda_\varphi \pi}} \tag{4}$$

Readily, on the left-hand side we get $\varphi \in \left\{ -\frac{(2n-1)\pi}{2n}, \cdots, -\frac{3\pi}{2n}, -\frac{\pi}{2n} \right\}$. The probability density function of φ on the left-hand side is

$$f_{left}(\varphi) = \begin{cases} \frac{1}{2} \cdot \frac{\lambda_\varphi e^{-\lambda_\varphi |\varphi|}}{1 - e^{-\lambda_\varphi \pi}}, & \varphi \in [-\pi, 0] \\ 0, & else \end{cases} \tag{5}$$

The probability that φ takes a specific value $\varphi_i = -\frac{(2|i|-1)\pi}{2n}$, $i = -n, \cdots, -2, -1$, is

$$Pr_{left}(\varphi = \varphi_i) = \frac{1}{2} \cdot \frac{e^{-\lambda_\varphi \frac{(|i|-1)\pi}{n}} - e^{-\lambda_\varphi \frac{|i|\pi}{n}}}{1 - e^{-\lambda_\varphi \pi}} \tag{6}$$

Summarizing Eqs. (4) and (6) we give the PDF of φ as

$$Pr(\varphi = \varphi_i) = \frac{1}{2} \cdot \frac{e^{-\lambda_\varphi \frac{(|i|-1)\pi}{n}} - e^{-\lambda_\varphi \frac{|i|\pi}{n}}}{1 - e^{-\lambda_\varphi \pi}} \tag{7}$$

$$i = -n, -(n-1), \cdots, -1, 1, \cdots, (n-1), n$$

2.4 Virtual Location Generation

When the actual location of a VANET user is $r = (0,0)$, a virtual location $r' = (d_j, \varphi_i)$ will be generated by deciding a distance d_j and an angle φ_i independently. The probability of generating $r' = (d_j, \varphi_i)$ can be given as

$$P(r'|r) = Pr(\varphi = \varphi_i) \cdot Pr(d = d_j) \tag{8}$$

3 Attack Model of Adversaries

In this section, we analyze the attack model of adversaries. We assume that the virtual location generation method designed in Sect. 2 is known by adversaries. The goal of adversaries is to infer the VANET user's location $\hat{r} = (\hat{d}, \hat{\varphi})$ based on its reported virtual location r'.

An adversary first formulates a polar coordinate system with r' being the reference point. Ideally, the adversary should take the moving direction of the VANET user as the reference direction. However, the VANET user does not send its moving direction to the LBS server and the adversary should estimate its moving direction based on the known r'. Assume that the adversary knows the regulated moving directions (RMDs) of all the lanes on the road. It will take the RMD of the lane that r' is on as the moving direction of the VANET user and the reference direction of the polar coordinate system.

In the formulated polar coordinate system, the adversary infers a location $\hat{r} = (\hat{d}_j, \hat{\varphi}_i)$ as the VANET user's actual location by deciding a distance $\hat{d}_j$ and an angle $\hat{\varphi}_i$ independently. Let $\hat{\varphi}_i$ denote the angle between $\hat{r}$ and r' in the adversary's polar coordinate system. When $\hat{\varphi}_i \geq 0$, the angle between r' and $\hat{r}$ in the VANET user's polar coordinate system is $-(\pi - \hat{\varphi}_i)$. When $\hat{\varphi}_i < 0$, the angle between r' and $\hat{r}$ in the VANET user's polar coordinate system is $\pi - |\hat{\varphi}_i|$. Since $Pr(\varphi = \varphi_j) = Pr(\varphi = -\varphi_j)$ according to the derivation in Sect. 2.3, it can be obtained that

$$Pr(\hat{\varphi} = \hat{\varphi}_i) = Pr(\varphi = \pi - |\hat{\varphi}_i|) \tag{9}$$

As for the distance between $\hat{r}$ and r', the distance between $\hat{r}$ and r' is $\hat{d}_j$ whether $\hat{\varphi}_i > 0$ or $\hat{\varphi}_i < 0$. Therefore, we can get

$$Pr(\hat{d} = \hat{d}_j) = = \frac{e^{-\lambda_d \frac{(j-1)d_{max}}{m}} - e^{-\lambda_d \frac{j d_{max}}{m}}}{1 - e^{-\lambda_d d_{max}}}, \quad j = 1, 2, \cdots, m \tag{10}$$

$$Pr(\hat{\varphi} = \hat{\varphi}_i) = \frac{1}{2} \cdot \frac{e^{-\lambda_\varphi(\pi - \frac{|i|\pi}{n})} - e^{-\lambda_\varphi(\pi - \frac{(|i|-1)\pi}{n})}}{1 - e^{-\lambda_\varphi \pi}} \tag{11}$$
$$i = -n, -(n-1), \cdots, -1, 1, \cdots, (n-1), n$$

Then, the attack model of the adversaries can be expressed as

$$A(\hat{r}|r') = Pr(\hat{\varphi} = \hat{\varphi}_i) \cdot Pr(\hat{d} = \hat{d}_j) \tag{12}$$

4   Performance Evaluation Metrics

In this section, two metrics are designed to evaluate the performance of the designed virtual location method from the perspectives of Qos loss and location privacy.

4.1   Qos Loss Metric

Compared with reporting the actual location to the LBS server, reporting the virtual location will lead to a Qos loss. The Qos loss goes higher when the virtual location goes further from the actual location in angle and/or distance. Therefore, the Qos loss for a specific virtual location $r'_{ij} = (d_j, \varphi_i)$ can be expressed as

$$Q_{ij} = \frac{|\varphi_i|}{\pi} + \frac{d_j}{d_{max}} \tag{13}$$

and the expected Qos loss of the designed virtual location generation method is

$$Q_{loss} = \sum_i \sum_j P(r'|r) Q_{ij} \tag{14}$$

4.2   Location Privacy Metric

We quantify the users location privacy as the adversarys expected error in his inference attack. According to (8) and (12), the location privacy performance of our design can be calculated as

$$Privacy = \sum_{r,r',\hat{r}} P(r'|r)A(\hat{r}|r')d_p(\hat{r}, r) \tag{15}$$

Here, r is the actual location of the VANET user, r' is the generated virtual location, $\hat{r}$ is the user's location estimated by the adversary, and $d_p(\hat{r}, r)$ is the Euclidean distance between $\hat{r}$ and r.

5   Numerical Analysis

In this section, we numerically analyze the scheme from the metrics of Qos loss and location privacy. Impacts of different parameters, including λ_φ, λ_d, m, n, and d_{max}, on the performance of the scheme are investigated. Two typical values 0.1 and 1 are taken for λ_φ indicating the case that $Pr(\varphi = \varphi_i)$ decreases slowly with the increase of $|i|$ and the case that $Pr(\varphi = \varphi_i)$ decreases sharply with the increase of $|i|$ respectively. Similarly, two typical values of λ_d are set to be 0.01 and 0.1. The values of d_{max} are set to be 100 m and 200 m corresponding to the cases where the VANET user has a relative high Qos requirement and a relative low Qos requirement respectively.

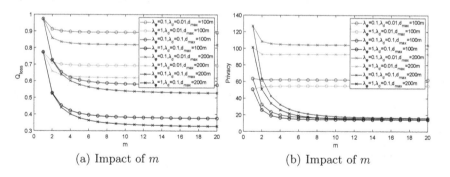

(a) Impact of m (b) Impact of m

Fig. 2. Impacts of m on Q_{loss} and $Privacy$

Figure 2 shows the impacts of m on Q_{loss} and $Privacy$. It can be seen that Q_{loss} and $Privacy$ decrease with the increase of m and the slope tends to be 0 when m is great enough (for example $m = 14$). When $m = 1$, the user can only take one value (i.e. $\frac{d_{max}}{2}$) for d. With the increase of m, the user has more options for d and it will choose smaller values with higher probabilities due to the properties of the exponential distribution. Therefore, the generated virtual

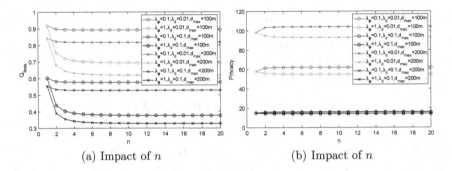

(a) Impact of n (b) Impact of n

Fig. 3. Impacts of n on Q_{loss} and $Privacy$

location goes closer to the actual location with the increase of m leading to a lower Q_{loss} and a lower $Privacy$. When m is great enough, the user tends to choose values for d continuously from the range of $[0, d_{max}]$. In this case, small impacts will be made on Q_{loss} and $Privacy$ with the increase of m resulting in a slope closing to 0. It can also be found that a lager d_{max} will lead to a lower Q_{loss} and a higher $Privacy$. A larger d_{max} indicates a lower Qos requirement, therefore the user is less sensitive to the Q_{loss} caused by the distance between the virtual location and the actual location. In this case, the user can generate a virtual location further from its actual location to gain higher privacy. As for the impacts of λ_φ and λ_d, it can be found that larger λ_φ and λ_d result in lower Q_{loss} and $Privacy$. The reason is that the user tends to generate virtual locations closer to the actual location in distance and angle with the increase of λ_φ and λ_d. This will lead to a lower Q_{loss} and $Privacy$.

The impacts of n on Q_{loss} and $Privacy$ are given in Fig. 3. The results shown in Fig. 3(a) can be explained similarly to that of Fig. 2(a). As for the results shown in Fig. 3(b), we found that λ_φ has no impact on $Privacy$ when $n = 1$ since the user always choose the value $\frac{\pi}{2}$ and $\frac{-\pi}{2}$ with equal probability. When n takes value no less than 2, no impact will be made on $Privacy$ by n since $Privacy$ defined in (15) in independent on the angle.

6   Conclusion

This paper proposes a location privacy protection scheme that generates virtual location by selecting angles and distances based on exponential probability distribution. A Qos loss metric and a location privacy metric are designed and used to numerically analyze the affects of different parameters on the performance of the proposed scheme. Simulation and experimental study of the proposed scheme will be conducted in our future work. Furthermore, we will combine virtual location generation with pseudonym change for better location privacy protection.

Acknowledgments. The authors would like to thank the support from the Natural Science Foundation of China (61802274, 61702056, 61602062), the Natural Science Fund for Colleges and Universities in Jiangsu Province (18KJB510044), the Natural Science Foundation of Jiangsu Province (BK20191475), and the Qing Lan Project of Jiangsu Province in China under grant No. 2019.

References

1. Cai, Z., He, Z., Guan, X., Li, Y.: Collective data-sanitization for preventing sensitive information inference attacks in social networks. IEEE Trans. Dependable Secure Comput. **15**(4), 577–590 (2016)
2. Cai, Z., Zheng, X., Yu, J.: A differential-private framework for urban traffic flows estimation via taxi companies. IEEE Trans. Ind. Inf. **15**(12), 6492–6499 (2019)
3. Chow, C.Y., Mokbel, M.F., Liu, X.: A peer-to-peer spatial cloaking algorithm for anonymous location-based service. In: 14th Annual ACM International Symposium on Advances in Geographic Information Systems, pp. 171–178 (2006)
4. Ghinita, G., Kalnis, P., Skiadopoulos, S.: MOBIHIDE: a mobilea peer-to-peer system for anonymous location-based queries. In: Papadias, D., Zhang, D., Kollios, G. (eds.) SSTD 2007. LNCS, vol. 4605, pp. 221–238. Springer, Heidelberg (2007). https://doi.org/10.1007/978-3-540-73540-3_13
5. Goyal, A.K., Agarwal, G., Tripathi, A.K.: Network architectures, challenges, security attacks, research domains and research methodologies in VANET: a survey. Int. J. Comput. Netw. Inf. Secur. **11**(10), 37–44 (2019)
6. He, Z., Cai, Z., Yu, J.: Latent-data privacy preserving with customized data utility for social network data. IEEE Trans. Veh. Technol. **67**(1), 665–673 (2017)
7. Khoshgozaran, A., Shahabi, C.: Blind evaluation of nearest neighbor queries using space transformation to preserve location privacy. In: Papadias, D., Zhang, D., Kollios, G. (eds.) SSTD 2007. LNCS, vol. 4605, pp. 239–257. Springer, Heidelberg (2007). https://doi.org/10.1007/978-3-540-73540-3_14
8. Kumar, V., Chand, N., Mishra, S.: Applications of VANETS: present & future. In: Communications and Network, vol. 05 (2013)
9. Lim, J., Yu, H., Kim, K., Kim, M., Lee, S.B.: Preserving location privacy of connected vehicles with highly accurate location updates. IEEE Commun. Lett. **21**(3), 540–543 (2016)
10. Mathews, S., Jinila, B.: An effective strategy for pseudonym generation & changing scheme with privacy preservation for VANET. In: International Conference on Electronics and Communication Systems, pp. 1–6 (2014)
11. Ni, W., Gu, M., Chen, X.: Location privacy-preserving k nearest neighbor query under users preference. Knowl.-Based Syst. **103**, 19–27 (2016)
12. Pan, Y., Li, J.: Cooperative pseudonym change scheme based on the number of neighbors in VANETS. J. Netw. Comput. Appl. **36**(6), 1599–1609 (2013)
13. Wang, J., Cai, Z., Yu, J.: Achieving personalized k-anonymity-based content privacy for autonomous vehicles in CPS. IEEE Trans. Ind. Inf. **16**(6), 4242–4251 (2019)
14. Wiedersheim, B., Ma, Z., Kargl, F., Papadimitratos, P.: Privacy in inter-vehicular networks: why simple pseudonym change is not enough. In: 7th International Conference on Wireless on-demand Network Systems and Services, pp. 176–183 (2010)
15. Wu, S., Liu, X.: Statistical properties of double censored exponential distribution. J. Mianyang Normal Univ. **31**(2), 13–15 (2012)

16. You, T., Peng, W., Lee, W.: Protecting moving trajectories with dummies. In: International Conference on Mobile Data Management, pp. 278–282 (2007)
17. Zeadally, S., Hunt, R., Chen, Y.S., Irwin, A., Hassan, A.: Vehicular ad hoc networks (VANETS): status, results, and challenges. Telecommun. Syst. **50**(4), 217–241 (2012). https://doi.org/10.1007/s11235-010-9400-5
18. Zhang, S., Mao, X., Choo, K.K.R., Peng, T., Wang, G.: A trajectory privacy-preserving scheme based on a dual-k mechanism for continuous location-based services. Inf. Sci. **527**, 406–419 (2020)
19. Zhang, X., Gui, X., Wu, Z.: Survey of privacy protection research for location services. J. Softw. **09**, 223–245 (2015)
20. Zheng, X., Cai, Z., Li, J., Gao, H.: Location-privacy-aware review publication mechanism for local business service systems. In: IEEE INFOCOM, pp. 1–9 (2017)

Reliable Visible Light-Based Underground Localization Utilizing a New Mechanism: Reverse Transceiver Position

Mingzhi Pang[1], Kuiyuan Zhang[1], Xu Yang[1], Yuqing Yin[1], Shouwan Gao[1,2], and Pengpeng Chen[1,2(✉)]

[1] School of Computer Science and Technology,
China University of Mining and Technology, Xuzhou 221116, China
{MingzPang,zhangkuiyuan,yang_xu,yinyuqing,gaoshouwan,chenp}@cumt.edu.cn
[2] China Mine Digitization Engineering Research Center, Ministry of Education,
Xuzhou 221116, China

Abstract. Traditional visible light-based positioning technology of deploying the receiver under the transmitter (i.e., LEDs deployed on the top and photodetectors deployed on the ground) in the mine tunnel is unreliable for optical signal reception and difficult to implement due to the complex mine tunnel environment such as occlusion of objects (e.g., Ore and Minecarts) on the ground. To address this issue, we propose a reliable visible light-based underground positioning algorithm that uses a novel reverse transceiver position mechanism, i.e., utilizing the existing miner's headlamp as the transmitter below and the photodiodes deployed on the top of the mine tunnel as the receiver above for broadcasting and receiving the light beacon representing miner's identity information. We determine the current location of each person through a series of base stations constructed by the receiver and achieve real-time positioning of all people combined with inertial navigation. We also overcome some technical challenges for this mechanism and the mine environment, including optimal frequency selection, robust frequency identification, and accurate base station positioning. The experiments show that the average positioning error of the base station is 0.06 m and the real-time location accuracy is 98% error of 2.5 m or less.

Keywords: Underground positioning · Visible light · Reverse position

1 Introduction

The attenuation of traditional wireless signals (e,g., infrared, ultrasonic, and some radio frequency (RF) signals such as RFID, ZigBee, and WiFi) is particularly serious in the underground mines [1], which makes the use of these wireless

This work was supported by the National Natural Science Foundation of China under Grant 51774282 and Grant 51904294.

D. Yu et al. (Eds.): WASA 2020, LNCS 12385, pp. 59–67, 2020.
https://doi.org/10.1007/978-3-030-59019-2_7

signals to locate personnel in the underground mines ineffective. Fortunately, visible light-based positioning technology provides a new idea for localization in underground mines with the advantages of less multipath effect, no electromagnetic effect, and strong resistance to electromagnetic interference [2–4]. However, traditional underground positioning technology based on visible light mostly locates person by deploying photodetectors on the mine tunnel ground, which is unreliable in terms of signal reception due to the limitations of the mine tunnel environment such as the obstruction of objects and the trampling of the miners.

Inspired by the essential lighting equipment for miners in the dark mine environment, we propose a reliable visible light-based underground positioning algorithm utilizing a new mechanism to reverse the position of the receiver and transmitter. The main idea of our algorithm is to innovatively utilize the miner's existing headlamp as the transmitter to send the miner's identity (ID) information and the photodiode (PD) deployed on the top of the mine tunnel is used as the receiver to perceive the mixed light signals. Just by constructing a series of base stations with the cheap PDs, we can accurately determine the base station where each miner arrives. Finally, we can achieve accurate real-time underground personnel positioning combined with the inertial navigation.

To improve the positioning accuracy and reliability of our algorithm in the harsh mine environment, we overcome two technical challenges: 1) there are a large number of miners in underground mines, which means that we need to select more frequencies to assign to each miner, and which also brings difficulties for recognizing the right visible light frequencies. Thus we design a set of frequency selection and identification methods for this problem. 2) when a miner walks with the headlamp on, a circular aperture will be left on the top of the mine tunnel, which causes the base station to perceive the miner's light beacon prematurely, even if this miner does not reach the location of the base station. To minimize the positioning error, we propose a frequency power tracking method to determine whether the miner is directly below the base station.

2   Algorithm Overview

Our algorithm is dedicated to resolving the problem of accurate personnel positioning in the underground mine scenario. Note that the actual underground mine is a long and narrow tunnel, so we can simplify the underground personnel positioning to one dimension and only locate the length of the tunnel that the miner walks. *Main idea.* Our algorithm is partitioned into two parts by default, namely the current position and the preliminary positioning. The preliminary positioning part refers to the initial judgment of the miner's position through the inertial navigation method. However, the positioning accuracy of single inertial navigation is poor due to the cumulative errors. Therefore, the positioning error is corrected by combining the current position part of the algorithm. The current position part refers to utilizing the base station to infer whether the miner is currently at the base station location. Next, we introduce how to accurately locate each miner's position by the base station in detail.

3   Locate Miners by Base Station

3.1   Frequency Selection

Prerequisite. We choose the pulse width modulation (PWM) to modulate each lamp blink at a unique frequency. Since PWM generates the square wave signal, we first perform Fourier series expansion on the square wave signal with period T. Suppose the amplitude of the square wave signal is A, the period and duty cycle are T and d, respectively. Thereby the flashing frequency f of the LED is $1/T$, and the time that the LED is on in one period is d/f. We substitute these parameters into the general Fourier series expansion of the even function, then the Fourier series expansion of the pulse waveform of a single LED light with a flashing frequency of f and a duty cycle of d is:

$$x(t) = Ad + \sum_{n=1}^{\infty} \frac{2A}{n\pi} sin(\pi n d) cos(2\pi n f t) \qquad (1)$$

where n is a positive integer greater than 0. Based on the Eq. 1 derived above, we next analyze the restrictions on the frequency selection separately in the following.

Duty Cycle. For an LED lamp with a PWM frequency, the duty cycle refers to the proportion of the time that the LED is on during a flashing cycle [5]. Notice that when duty cycle d is 50%, we can see from Eq. 1 that there are no harmonics when n is even (i.e., $sin\frac{\pi n}{2} = 0$). It indicates that the number of harmonics is reduced to half when the duty cycle is 50%. Hence, we select a 50% duty cycle for the PWM by considering the number of harmonics.

Threshold of Flashing Frequency. First, the prior research shows that when the flashing frequency of LEDs is greater than 1000 Hz, the humanly perceivable picker can be completely avoided [6]. Second, the Nyquist Shannon sampling theorem states that the sampling rate must be greater than twice the highest frequency of the signal to retain the information in the original signal and avoid the problem of signal waveform distortion [7]. Finally, we conclude that the selected frequency range is between 1000 Hz and $R/2$, where R is the sampling rate.

Threshold of the Interval Between Adjacent Frequencies. When performing FFT on the sampling data (see Sect. 3.2), we must consider both the frequency resolution and the mutual interference between adjacent frequencies. Frequency resolution refers to the smallest interval that the server can identify the power peaks of two adjacent frequencies. Suppose the sampling number is N and the sampling rate is R, thereby the frequency resolution is R/N. Moreover, the previous work shows that the lowest adjacent frequency interval has to be above 200 Hz to ensure the robust frequency separation [8,9]. Therefore, suppose the frequency resolution is $f_{resolution}$, we set the threshold of the interval between adjacent frequencies as $Max(f_{resolution}, 200)$.

3.2   Frequency Identification

We introduce a reliable light frequency identification method for the mine environment in this subsection. We divide this frequency identification method into three parts: data sampling, FFT and band-pass filter processing, and frequency matching. The specific process is as follows.

First of all, the system continuously samples the output voltage of a series of PDs in the sampling times (suppose the sampling rate is R and the sampling number is N, thereby a sampling time is N/R), and then stores the sampled data in the database. *Secondly,* FFT is performed on the sampled data to obtain the spectrum of the mixed optical signals sensed by the PDs, in which the spectrum contains all visible light frequencies and corresponding power values. Then the band-pass filter to remove frequencies that are not within the preset frequency range of miners. Since the frequencies assigned to the miners are known, we can easily filter out other frequencies that do not fall within the preset frequency range with the help of the band-pass filter. *Finally,* there may still be other frequency power peaks in the reserved frequency range. For this problem, we only need to match the reserved frequencies with the preset frequency dataset of the miners to recognize the correct frequencies.

3.3   Frequency Power Tracking

When the light source under a certain spotlight angle vertically hits the plane, a circular aperture will be left on the plane. Figure 1(a) illustrates an aperture of radius v when an LED light with a spotlight angle α irradiates on a plane with the vertical distance u. We can deduce the expression for v is as follows:

$$v = u \tan \alpha, 0 < \alpha < \frac{\pi}{2} \tag{2}$$

From Eq. 2, it is clear that the radius v of the aperture is determined by u and α, and both have a positive correlation with v. Similarly, we can also infer that the maximum horizontal distance that the base station can detect the optical signals emitted by miners is v, which means that the base station has a maximum error of v in locating miners. Therefore the law of illumination is used in our algorithm to minimize the positioning error.

The law of illumination says that when illuminating with a point light source, the illumination on an object's surface perpendicular to the light is inversely proportional to the square of the distance between the illuminated face and the light source [10]. In other words, the illumination on the PD is related to the distance between the miner's headlamp and the base station. Thus we can accurately determine the position of miners based on this principle. As Fig. 1(b) shows in 2D, when the miner is in position A, the PD of the base station senses the optical signals emitted by a miner's headlamp for the first time. We can regard β as the basis to judge the degree of the miner approaching the base station. When the maximum value of β is α, the PD receives the light signals emitted by the miner for the first time. As the horizontal distance between the miner and the base station continues to decrease, the value of β also continues to decrease until it tends to 0. On the contrary, the illumination on the PD keeps increasing and when $\beta = 0$ (i.e., the miner is just under the base station), the illumination E reaches the maximum value. Then we can think that when the illuminance of the base station reaches the maximum, the miner just walks to the base station position. Notice that the direct positive correlation between the output voltage and the perceived mixed light intensity of PD, the frequency power at frequency f_i is approximately proportional to the intensity of the light rays flashing at f_i after frequency separation [11]. So we can determine the position of multiple miners at the same time by monitoring the power values of each miner's beacon frequency.

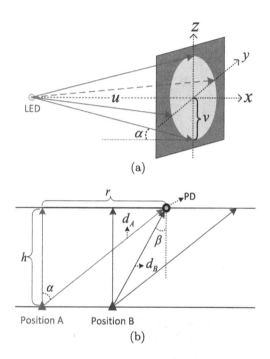

Fig. 1. (a) The aperture left when the light is irradiated on the plane. (b) The relationship between the miner's different positions and the illumination values of PD.

4   Algorithm Experiments

4.1   Experimental Device and Environment

Transmitter. Figure 2 shows a transmitter used to generate optical signals of different beacon frequencies. It includes multiple commercial LED lights, one self-made LED driver, and an FPGA. First, the LED luminaire has a rated power of 7 W and a 15-degree spotlight angle. Second, the self-made LED driver is used to supply power to all LEDs. Finally, based on our existing conditions, we select ZYNQ-7020 FPGA as the modulator for PWM frequency and duty cycle modulation of these LEDs.

Receiver. As shown in Fig. 3, the receiver consists of two parts: the perception part and the sampling part. First, the perception part is composed of an integrated module and the module driver, where the integrated module is cascaded with a PD (Honeywell SD5421-002) and a resistor (10 KΩ). Second, the sampling part composed of ZYNQ-7020 FPGA and AN706 analog-to-digital converter (ADC) to sample and process the voltage data output by PD.

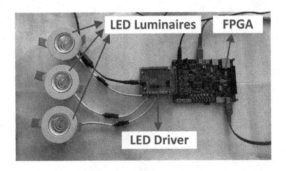

Fig. 2. Transmitter

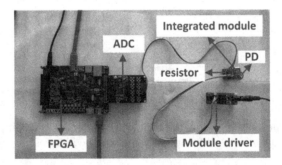

Fig. 3. Receiver

Experimental Scenarios. Since the underground of the mine is a long and dark tunnel, so we think of utilizing the indoor corridor to simulate the underground environment. The height of our indoor corridor is 2.5m, which is close to the height of the underground mines.

4.2   Algorithm Evaluation

Frequency Identification of Multiple Miners. We now evaluate the performance of frequency identification when there are multiple miners within the base station's perception range. Six LED lights are utilized for this experiment considering the limitation of the size of underground mines. We can see from Fig. 4 that seven different visible light frequencies with distinct power peaks are separated, and the six preset frequencies can be successfully recognized through the frequency matching method.

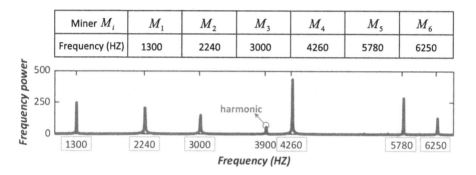

Fig. 4. Frequency separation effect of six miners.

Positioning Accuracy. *Positioning Accuracy of the Base Station.* To verify the accuracy of base station positioning miners, four users (different height and speed) participated in our experiment. They respectively wear the modulated LED light with 2500 Hz frequency to advance towards the base station in the dark corridor, and then we use the receiver to sample the real-time optical signal. We compared the position of each miner at the maximum frequency power with the position directly below the base station. As Fig. 5 shows, we can calculate the average positioning error of the base station is no more than 0.06 m. This indicates that our base station can accurately locate the miners.

Combining with Inertial Navigation. In our previous work in [12], we have proposed an inertial navigation method combining step length calculation and step detection by the accelerometer. Moreover, the experiments verify that the error of the step detection method is less than 2.3%, indicating that it has a good performance in the mine. Therefore, we still continue this inertial navigation method in this article. Then combined with our base station of visible light for error correction, we can achieve a real-time localization error 98.7% of 2.5 m or less.

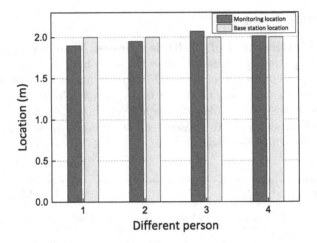

Fig. 5. Positioning accuracy of the base station.

5   Conclusion

Aiming to solve the problem of unreliable signal reception of traditional visible light-based underground positioning algorithms due to the deployment of receivers on the complex environment of the tunnel ground, we present a reliable visible light-based underground positioning algorithm that utilizes a novel reverse transceiver position mechanism, i.e., utilizing the existing miner's headlamp as the transmitter below and the PDs deployed on the top of the mine tunnel as the receiver. Then our algorithm uses visible light technology to establish a series of base stations to accurately locate the current position of miners, and then combines inertial navigation to achieve accurate real-time positioning of miners. The experimental results show that our algorithm achieves the average positioning error of the base station is 0.06 m, and the real-time underground personnel positioning error 98.7% of 2.5 m.

References

1. Farjow, W., Raahemifar, K., Fernando, X.: Novel wireless channels characterization model for underground mines. Appl. Math. Model. **39**(19), 5997–6007 (2015)
2. Huang, C., Zhang, X.: Impact and feasibility of darklight led on indoor visible light positioning system. In: 2017 IEEE 17th International Conference on Ubiquitous Wireless Broadband (ICUWB), pp. 1–5. IEEE (2017)
3. Singh, S., Kakamanshadi, G., Gupta, S.: Visible light communication-an emerging wireless communication technology. In: 2015 2nd International Conference on Recent Advances in Engineering & Computational Sciences (RAECS), pp. 1–3. IEEE (2015)
4. Zhou, X., Campbell, A.T.: Visible light networking and sensing. In: Proceedings of the 1st ACM Workshop on Hot Topics in Wireless, pp. 55–60 (2014)

5. Lee, K., Park, H.: Modulations for visible light communications with dimming control. IEEE Photonics Technol. Lett. **23**(16), 1136–1138 (2011)
6. Kuo, Y.S., Pannuto, P., Hsiao, K.J., Dutta, P.: Luxapose: indoor positioning with mobile phones and visible light. In: Proceedings of the 20th Annual International Conference on Mobile Computing and Networking, pp. 447–458 (2014)
7. Jerri, A.J.: The Shannon sampling theorem–its various extensions and applications: A tutorial review. Proc. IEEE **65**(11), 1565–1596 (1977)
8. Yang, F., Li, S., Yang, Z., Qian, C., Gu, T.: Spatial multiplexing for non-line-of-sight light-to-camera communications. IEEE Trans. Mob. Comput. **18**(11), 2660–2671 (2018)
9. Li, T., An, C., Tian, Z., Campbell, A.T., Zhou, X.: Human sensing using visible light communication. In: Proceedings of the 21st Annual International Conference on Mobile Computing and Networking, pp. 331–344 (2015)
10. Murdoch, J.B.: Inverse square law approximation of illuminance. J. Illum. Eng. Soc. **10**(2), 96–106 (1981)
11. Li, T., Xiong, X., Xie, Y., Hito, G., Yang, X.D., Zhou, X.: Reconstructing hand poses using visible light. Proc. ACM Interact. Mob. Wearable Ubiquit. Technol. **1**(3), 1–20 (2017)
12. Niu, Q., Yang, X., Yin, Y.: IPL: image-assisted person localization for underground coal mines. Sensors **18**(11), 3679 (2018)

Research on 5G Internet of Vehicles Facilities Based on Coherent Beamforming

Juan Xu[1], Lan Wu[1], Lei Shi[1(✉)], Yi Shi[2], and Wenwen Zhou[1]

[1] School of Computer Science and Information Engineering,
HeFei University of Technology, Hefei 230009, China
shilei@hfut.edu.cn
[2] Intelligent Automation Inc., 15400 Calhoun Drive, Rockville, MD 20855, USA

Abstract. As an important application scenario of edge computing, the Internet of Vehicles (IoV) is a special wireless network which needs a serious requirement on communication speed and latency. Nowadays, the 5G wireless networks have been put into commercial use, which makes IoV's higher speed and lower latency requirements possible. However, comparing with 4G base station, the cost of 5G base station is very high, while its cover range is small. These weaknesses make 5G wireless network difficult to be used directly on IoV. Fortunately, Coherent Beamforming (CB) technology makes the long distance transmission possible in 5G wireless network. While as a new technology in communication, few works has been done on considering to use it on IoV. In this paper, we consider to use CB on IoV scenario. We aim to give an optimal scheme for deploying the roadside CB-nodes so that we can transmit data to the edge server with a low cost. We first give the mathematical model and clarify that it is an NP-hard model. Then we design a heuristic algorithm for solving the problem. We call our algorithm as the Iterative Coherent Beamforming Node Design (ICBND) algorithm. Simulation results show that the ICBND algorithm can greatly reduce the cost of communication network infrastructure.

Keywords: Coherent Beamforming · Edge computing · Internet of Vehicles · 5G

1 Introduction

As people's pursuit of comfort and safety keeps improving, the research about Internet of Vehicles (IoV) receives much attention and has been studied more [1–3]. Especially in recent years with the development of artificial intelligence technology, people have paid much attention to automatic driving technology. Autonomous driving technology relies much on the development of the vehicles

This article was supported by the National Natural Science Foundation of China (Grant No. 61806067) and Key Research and Development Project in Anhui Province (Grant No. 201904a06020024).

D. Yu et al. (Eds.): WASA 2020, LNCS 12385, pp. 68–77, 2020.
https://doi.org/10.1007/978-3-030-59019-2_8

communicating ability with their surroundings. As a hot research field, edge computing, which sinks a large number of complex calculations into the edge server environment, thus makes automatic driving technology possible [4], and plays an important role in autonomous driving [5,6], Internet of things (IoT) [7] and other research fields [8–10]. The basic communication of the edge computing framework is built on the 5G network. 5G has characteristics of high data volume and low latency [11]. In addition to bringing more extreme experience and larger capacity, 5G technology is now widely discussed in smart grids, interconnected vehicles, autonomous driving and surgery [13], and will open the era of the IoV and penetrate into various industries [12]. However, compared with current commercial 4G technology, 5G also have disadvantages. The coverage of 5G base station (BS) is small and the cost is high [14]. Due to the wide range of automobile work scenarios, it is difficult for 5G to directly replace the 4G based vehicle networking system. Fortunately, in recent years, the communication technology based on coherent beamforming (CB) has provided the possibility of large-scale data communication.

CB technique needs multiple nodes work together for increasing the transmission range. When CB technology is used for transmitting, each node will use one omnidirectional antenna. In [15], the authors have proved that the power gain of N senders and M receivers in CB communication can reach to N^2M. Nowadays some studies about CB have been done, but most are focused on power and delay issues. For example, in [16], the authors designed an open-loop CB scheme for MISO communications. In [17], the authors proposed an adaptive beamforming to improve the contrast to noise ratio. In [18], CB was applied to the radar system, so that the MIMO radar can meet the spatial domain transmit beamforming constraints.

To our knowledge, most predecessors use CB technology to study network throughput and power problems. We are the first to explore the application of CB technology in 5G vehicle networking. We try to expand the communication range and reduce the number of base stations so as to reduce the cost without reducing the communication requirements of vehicles. In this paper, we analyze the working model of CB in 5G vehicle network. We place CB-nodes reasonably and effectively on both sides of the road. These CB-nodes can collaborate to help the vehicle transfer data to the edge server. Compared with 5G base station layout, the delay of this method is similar to the layout of 4G base stations, which greatly reduces the cost of infrastructure.

The rest of the article is organized as follows. In Sect. 2, we give the system model and algorithm. The designed model is a NP-hard problem, and it is difficult to find the optimal solution directly. Then we design a heuristic algorithm for Iterative Coherent Beamforming Node Design (ICBND) based on greedy strategy to find the optimal number of nodes in each subpart, and obtain the approximate optimal solution by combining the optimal value of each subpart. In Sect. 3, we give a comparison experiment, and propose a control variable method to compare the simulation results of the two methods. In Sect. 4, we give the conclusion.

2   System Model and Problem Definition

We first describe the system model (see Fig. 1). Consider a part of straight road with the length L. An edge server is located on the road side, near the center point of the road. A number of wireless nodes are placed on both sides of the road for helping communicating. When a vehicle is passing the road, it will communicate with the edge server by the help of these nodes. The vehicle will first broadcast data to its nearby nodes, and then these nodes will collaborate to send data to the edge server by using the CB technique. We call these nodes as CB-nodes. Suppose the vehicle need to transmit D data to the edge server, and suppose it will pass the road by T time. We want to give an optimal scheme for deploying CB-nodes, so that we can use a minimum number of CB-nodes while guaranteeing that the vehicle can finish its transmission job in T time. When different vehicles pass the road, they may have different speed and different transmission requirement. This may lead different optimal solutions. So we suppose we design the optimal solution for the vehicle with the maximum speed (which leads a minimum passing time T) and the maximum transmission requirement (which leads a maximum data D).

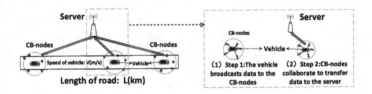

Fig. 1. CB-nodes collaborates with the vehicle to transmit data.

2.1   Network Layer Model and Problem Formulation

Denote s_i as one of the CB-node, denote N as the set of all CB-nodes, i.e., $s_i \in N$, and denote n as the number of N. In the scheduling time T, the whole Data D may be divided into several pieces and several different CB-nodes may collaborate for each transmission. Denote S_j as one group of CB-nodes that collaborate for a transmission, denote M as the set of all CB-node groups, i.e., $S_j \in M$, and denote m as the number of M. Apparently $m \ll 2^n - 1$. Notice that one CB-node s_i may be in different groups. Denote $D(S_j)$ as the data of S_j's transmission, we have

$$D = \sum_{j=1}^{m} D(S_j). \tag{1}$$

One transmission has two stages. First, the vehicle broadcasts data to its nearby CB-nodes. Second, CB-nodes transmit data to the edge server. For the first stage, denote binary variables $x_{s_i}(t)$ and $x_{S_j}(t)$ to indicate if s_i or S_j receives the vehicle's broadcasting data at time t, i.e., if $x_{s_i}(t) = 1$ (or $x_{s_j}(t) = 1$), it means that s_i (or S_j) will receive data at time t. For the second stage, similar to the first stage, we will denote binary variables $y_{s_i}(t)$ and $y_{s_j}(t)$. Then we have

$$x_{s_i}(t) \geq x_{s_j}(t) \text{ and } y_{s_i}(t) \geq y_{s_j}(t) \quad (\forall i, s_i \in S_j, 0 \leq t \leq T), \tag{2}$$

For s_i (or S_j), it can only receives or transmits data at time t, we have

$$x_{s_i}(t) + y_{s_i}(t) \leq 1 \text{ and } x_{s_j}(t) + y_{s_j}(t) \leq 1. \tag{3}$$

Only one group can receive the broadcasting data at time t, and only one group can transmit to the edge server at time t, we have

$$\sum_{S_j \in M} x_{s_j}(t) \leq 1 \text{ and } \sum_{S_j \in M} y_{s_j}(t) \leq 1. \tag{4}$$

Denote P_v as the transmission power of the vehicle, then the vehicle's transmission range can be formulated as $R_v = \sqrt[\lambda]{(P_v/\beta N_0)}$, where N_0 is the noise power, λ is the pass loss index, and β is a constant. We can get similar formulation about a single CB-node's transmission range $R_s = \sqrt[\lambda]{(P_s/\beta N_0)}$, where we suppose all CB-nodes have the same transmission power P_s. Denote $\sigma_{v \to s_i}^{S_j}(t)$ as the signal-to-noise-ratio (SINR) from the vehicle to s_i of the set S_j at time t, denote $d_{v \to s_i}(t)$ as the distance between the vehicle and s_i at time t, we have

$$\sigma_{v \to s_i}^{S_j}(t) = \frac{P_v d_{v \to s_i}^{-\lambda}(t) \cdot x_{s_j}(t)}{N_0} \geq \beta \cdot x_{s_j}(t) \quad (s_i \in S_j, S_j \in M). \tag{5}$$

Denote $\sigma_{s_j \to b}(t)$ as the sum of SINR from all CB-nodes in S_j for sending data to the edge server at time t, and denote $d_{s_i \to b}$ as the distance between s_i and the edge server. Since we use the CB technique for transmissions, which means several CB-nodes will cooperate for transmitting, we have

$$\sigma_{s_j \to b}(t) = \frac{P_s \left(\sum_{s_i \in S_j} \sqrt{d_{s_i \to b}^{-\lambda}} \right)^2 \cdot y_{s_j}(t)}{N_0} \geq \beta \cdot y_{s_j}(t) \quad (S_j \in M). \tag{6}$$

Denote $r_{v \to s_i}^{S_j}(t)$ as the vehicle's transmitting data rate to s_i of the set S_j at time t, and denote $r_{s_j \to b}(t)$ as the transmitting data rate from the set S_j to the edge server at time t. Denote W as the bandwidth. Since the transmitting data rate should not be larger than the channel capacity, we have

$$r_{v \to s_i}^{S_j}(t) \leq W \log_2(1 + \sigma_{v \to s_i}^{S_j}(t)) \quad (s_i \in S_j, S_j \in M, 0 \leq t \leq T), \tag{7}$$

$$r_{s_j \to b}(t) \leq W \log_2(1 + \sigma_{s_j \to b}(t)) \quad (S_j \in M, 0 \leq t \leq T). \tag{8}$$

Consider the relationship between the transmitting data rate and the transmitting data of a set S_j, and the second step, we have

$$D(S_j) = \int_{t=0}^{T} r_{v \to s_i}^{S_j}(t)dt = \int_{t=0}^{T} r_{S_j \to b}(t)dt \quad (s_i \in S_j, S_j \in M, 0 \le t \le T). \quad (9)$$

$$\int_{t=0}^{\eta} r_{v \to s_i}^{S_j}(t)dt \ge \int_{t=0}^{\eta} r_{S_j \to b}(t)dt \quad (s_i \in S_j, S_j \in M, 0 < \eta \le T). \quad (10)$$

Denote n_{max} as the maximum number of roadside CB-nodes arranged on. Apparent if we deploy enough CB-nodes by the roadside the vehicle will always complete the communication properly. So suppose we first deploy enough CB-nodes by the roadside, then we try to find nodes which are not used in the whole scheduling time as many as possible, we will get the optimal solution. That is, we are trying to find CB-nodes s_i that satisfies $y_{s_i}(t) = 0$ when each vehicle passes through the entire road. We can set a binary variable z_i

$$z_i = \begin{cases} 1 : \exists & y_{s_i}(t) = 1, 0 \le t \le T \\ 0 : \forall & y_{s_i}(t) = 0, 0 \le t \le T. \end{cases} \quad (11)$$

Based on the above discussions, we can get the final formula,

$$\begin{aligned} &\min \sum_{i=1}^{n_{max}} z_i \\ &\text{s.t. } (1), (2) - (11). \end{aligned} \quad (12)$$

However, notice that in (12), we do not know which specific CB-node in each set S_j, and the number of all sets m may be a very large number. We also notice that $x_{s_i}(t)$, $y_{S_j}(t)$ are continuous variables about time t, which means we have infinite variables. So (12) cannot be solved directly.

2.2   Problem Refinement

In Sect. 2.1, we give the problem formulation. In this sub section, we will give the problem model reformulation. Notice that for (12), we divide the whole data D into many small parts $D(S_j)$, and for each part we use a different CB-node-set S_j for serving it. If we can design an algorithm for establishing S_j, then we may find a way to solve (12). To do that, we need to answer three problems. (i), How many parts we should divided at least for D? (ii), For each S_j, how many nodes should be included in? (iii), Are there any CB-nodes in different S_j?

For the first problem, notice that the vehicle usually travel with a constant speed and we assume that the vehicle has a speed v in time T. We have $v \le v_{max} = \frac{L}{T}$. Define the amount of data sent by each part as $D(S_j)$. Since the time of each vehicle's transmission is the time when the vehicle passes through the CB-node's transmission range, (i.e, $2R_s$), we should ensure that the vehicle completes the transmission within $\frac{2R_s}{v_{max}}$ time. Assume that the CB-node's transmission range in each segment is not intersected with the other segments, we will equally divide the whole road for $h \geq h_{min} = \frac{L}{2R_s}$ parts at least. In each path part l_j, we will arrange a set S_j for transmitting $D(S_j)$ to the edge server. We also notice that when the vehicle enters a path part, the distance between it and the CB-nodes in this part will not change too much. So we can consider $d_{v \to s_i}(t)$ as a constant d_v, and the data transmission rate $r^{S_j}_{v \to s_i}$ as a constant r_v.

For the second problem, the needed CB-nodes number is decided by the distance between the edge server and each set, and now we have known S_j is arranged for l_j. Denote the distance as $d(S_j)$. Denote the needed number of CB-nodes as $n(S_j)$. We have

$$n(S_j) = \lceil \frac{d(S_j)}{R_s} \rceil. \tag{13}$$

Since we consider the vehicle has a constant speed v, and the road is divided equally, so the vehicle will pass each road path part with a same time slot length. Denote time slot as $t_i (i = 1, 2, ..., h)$. We have $t_1 = t_2 = \cdots = t_h$. Then we have,

$$D(S_j) = \frac{D}{h} = r_v \cdot t_j \leq W \log_2(1 + \sigma^{S_j}_{v \to s_i}(t_j)) \cdot t_j. \tag{14}$$

Based on the first discussion and the second discussion, we can get a feasible solution, only if we put enough CB-nodes in each CB-node-set. The result of the third problem is affected by the length of the segment and the propagation range of the CB-node. We refer to the same CB-node in different set of CB-nodes as a cross-bit CB-node. In the following, we set up the ICBND algorithm. According to the number of segments, we get the minimum number of CB-nodes needed for each segment to work separately, and calculate the number of cross-bit CB-nodes. We remove repeated CB-nodes to obtain the optimal total number of CB-nodes. The specific steps are described in the next sub section.

2.3   Algorithms

For the third problem, we notice the whole road has been divided into $h(h_{min} \leq h \leq h_{max})$ path parts. Since the vehicle has a permanent transmission range R_v, it is easy to find that with the different number of road path parts, several CB-node-sets can be in one vehicle's transmission range (see Fig. 2). In these situations, in order to describe the problem more conveniently, if we put the cross-bit CB-nodes in the common parts, we will save more CB-nodes. Based on these discussions, we try to propose our heuristic algorithm. The main idea of our algorithm is based on iterative steps. We call our algorithm as the Iterative Coherent Beamforming Node Design (ICBND) algorithm. In the following we give the main four steps of the ICBND algorithm.

First, initialization h_{max}, h_{min}, etc. Determine the road is divided into h segment, and calculate the distance from the center of each segment to the edge server. Then, the number of CB-nodes required for each segment individually is calculated according to Eq. (11), and the number of CB-nodes required for each segment is temporarily stored in an array.

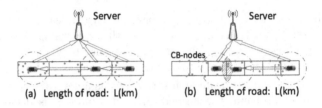

(a) Length of road: L(km)   (b) Length of road: L(km)

Fig. 2. CB-nodes layout scheme.

Second, input the broadcast range and segment length of the CB-node and calculate the number of cross-bit CB-nodes in each segment.

Third, each segment has at least one receiving CB-node, and other CB-nodes can be placed on the intersection of the two segments.

Fourth, add the minimum number of CB-nodes for each segment.

Algorithm 1. Algorithm for Iterative Coherent Beamforming Node Design

---

Require: Initializing h_{min},h_{max}; initial the CB-nodes $sum = 0$;
1: initial $x = 0$, $j = 1$, $h = h_{min}$;
2: **repeat**
3:     **repeat**
4:         Calculate the distance between S_j and the edge server: $d(S_j)$;
5:         Calculate the number of CB-nodes in the each region: $n(S_j) = \lceil \frac{d(S_j)}{R_s} \rceil$;
6:         Determine the relation between R_s the value between h_{min} and h_{max} , then calculate that the same CB-node exists in several different sets of CB-nodes;
7:         Calculate x, $n(S_j) = n(S_j) - x$;
8:         $sum = sum + n(S_j)$;
9:     **until** The vehicle ran the last part of the road, $j = h$;
10:     get one kind of task assignment scheme
11: **until** $h = h_{max}$;
12: select the best assignment scheme to be the assignment scheme for this time slice;

---

3   Simulation

In this section, we will give simulation results. We first give a specific layout scheme for a particular network, and then give the comparison results of more network schemes. We set the straight-line distance between the edge server and the road is $a = 100$ m. The noise power N_0 is 10^{-7} W, and the road strength loss factor $\lambda = 3$. The total bandwidth of road strength $W = 3.5$ GHz. Denote the vehicle's broadcast range as the CB-node's broadcast range.

3.1   A Special Case with CB-nodes Layout

In this section, under the condition that the road length is $L = 4$ km. the transmission power P_s of the CB-node is 0.3 W, and the broadcast radius is

$R_s = 144$ m. According to the algorithm 1 execution results, the data with cross-bit CB-nodes from 98 to 173, and the data without cross-bit CB-nodes from 154 to 462. the total number of with cross-bit CB-nodes is always less than the total number of without cross-bit CB-nodes, so the scheme with cross-bit CB-nodes has advantages. According to the data, the total number of optimal CB-nodes is 98. Based on this, we adopt the optimal CB-nodes layout scheme to simulate the layout of real road CB-nodes, as shown in Fig. 3.

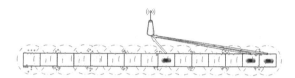

Fig. 3. The optimal CB-nodes layout scheme in a specific scenario.

According to market research, we set the cost of a CB-node at \$15 and the cost of a 5G base station at \$28000. For normal communication, a 5G base station needs to be deployed every 200 m. The data shows that the optimal scheme is 98 CB-nodes and one edge server, and the cost is \$29470. The length of the road is $L = 4$ km, so 20 5G base stations are needed and the cost is about \$560000. So, we could save about \$530530 based on our planned layout.

3.2 General Case

In this section, we give more experimental results for different parameter settings. We let L change from 2 km to 8 km, with the step 1 km, and let P_s change from 0.2 W to 0.5 W, with the step 0.1 W. Then we can calculate different R_s as 126 m, 144 m, 159 m and 170 m. Based on these settings, we can get a series of results, as shown in Fig. 4.

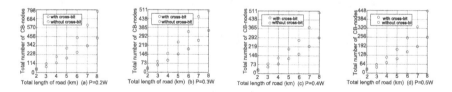

Fig. 4. Different number of CB-nodes needed under different L and P_s.

As shown in Fig. 4, data with cross-bit CB-nodes scheme is always better than data without cross-bit CB-nodes scheme. Then, we compare the scheme with cross-bit CB-nodes scheme with the 5G base station scheme. In detail, as shown in Fig. 4(b), when $P_s = 0.2$ W, the optimal number of CB-nodes that needed with the cross-bit scheme in different L are 28, 60, 98, 150, 192, 262 and 342, respectively. The corresponding costs are approximately $28420, $28900, $29470, $30250, $30880, $31930 and $33130. When L values from 2 km to 8 km, with the step 1 km, the number of 5G base stations from 10 to 40, with the step 5. The corresponding costs from $280000 to $1120000, with the step $140000. Therefore, adopting our method can greatly reduce the cost of infrastructure.

4 Conclusion

In this work, we study the use of coherent beamforming technology on IoV scenario. We build a general model for this problem, with the goal of reducing the communication cost as much as possible while satisfying the transmission conditions. Since the designed model is NP-hard problem, we propose an effective heuristic algorithm ICBND, it using the iterative method to calculate the total number of the least CB-nodes on the whole road. In the simulation experiment, we compared the scheme with cross-bit CB-node, the scheme without cross-bit CB-node and the scheme of 5G base station layout, comparative experiments show that our algorithm has low cost performance.

References

1. Cai, Z., Zheng, X., Yu, J.: A differential-private framework for urban traffic flows estimation via taxi companies. IEEE Trans. Ind. Inform. **15**(12), 6492–6499 (2019)
2. Xiong, Z., Li, W., Han, Q., Cai, Z.: Privacy-preserving auto-driving: a GAN-based approach to protect vehicular camera data. In: 2019 IEEE International Conference on Data Mining (ICDM), pp. 668–677 (2019)
3. Guan, X., Huang, Y., Cai, Z., Ohtsuki, T.: Intersection-based forwarding protocol for vehicular ad hoc networks. Telecommun. Syst. **62**(1), 67–76 (2015). https://doi.org/10.1007/s11235-015-9983-y
4. Hou, X., et al.: Reliable computation offloading for edge computing-enabled software-defined IoV. IEEE Internet Things J. **7**, 7097–7111 (2020)
5. Xie, R., Tang, Q., Wang, Q., Liu, X., Yu, F.R., Huang, T.: Collaborative vehicular edge computing networks: architecture design and research challenges. IEEE Access **7**, 178942–178952 (2019)
6. Wang, J., Cai, Z., Yu, J.: Achieving personalized k-anonymity-based content privacy for autonomous vehicles in CPS. IEEE Trans. Ind. Inform. **16**(6), 4242–4251 (2020)
7. Na, W., Jang, S., Lee, Y., Park, L., Dao, N., Cho, S.: Frequency resource allocation and interference management in mobile edge computing for an internet of things system. IEEE Internet Things J. **6**(3), 4910–4920 (2019)
8. Xu, X., Zhang, X., Liu, X., Jiang, J., Qi, L., Bhuiyan, M.Z.A.: Adaptive computation offloading with edge for 5G-envisioned internet of connected vehicles. IEEE Trans. Intell. Transp. Syst. (2020). https://doi.org/10.1109/TITS.2020.2982186
9. LiWang, M., Dai, S., Gao, Z., Du, X., Guizani, M., Dai, H.: A computation offloading incentive mechanism with delay and cost constraints under 5G satellite-ground IoV architecture. IEEE Wirel. Commun. **26**(4), 124–132 (2019)

10. Zhang, L., Cao, W.J., Zhang, X.X., Xu, H.T.: Mac(2): enabling multicasting and congestion control with multichannel transmission for intelligent vehicle terminal in internet of vehicles. Int. J. Distrib. Sens. Netw. **14**(8) (2018). https://doi.org/10.1177/1550147718793586
11. Shah, S.A.A., Ahmed, E., Imran, M., Zeadally, S.: 5G for vehicular communications. IEEE Commun. Mag. **56**(1), 111–117 (2018)
12. Gupta, A., Jha, R.K.: A survey of 5G network: architecture and emerging technologies. IEEE Access **3**, 1206–1232 (2015)
13. Li, S.C., Xu, L.D., Zhao, S.: 5G internet of things: a survey. J. Ind. Inf. Integr. **10**, 1–9 (2018)
14. Cheng, X., Chen, C., Zhang, W., Yang, Y.: 5G-enabled cooperative intelligent vehicular (5GenCIV) framework: when Benz meets Marconi. IEEE Intell. Syst. **32**(3), 53–59 (2017)
15. Shi, Y., Sagduyu, Y.E.: Coherent communications in self-organizing networks with distributed beamforming. IEEE Trans. Veh. Technol. **69**(1), 760–770 (2020)
16. Nanzer, J.A., Schmid, R.L., Comberiate, T.M., Hodkin, J.E.: Open-loop coherent distributed arrays. IEEE Trans. Microw. Theory Tech. **65**(5), 1662–1672 (2017)
17. Bai, C., Zhang, X., Qiao, X., Sang, Y., Wan, M.: Ultrasound transcranial imaging based on fast coherent-time-delay and correlative pixel-based beamforming. In: IEEE International Ultrasonics Symposium (2018)
18. Deng, H., Geng, Z., Himed, B.: MIMO radar waveform design for transmit beamforming and orthogonality. IEEE Trans. Aerosp. Electron. Syst. **52**(3), 1421–1433 (2016)

LPE-RCM: Lightweight Privacy-Preserving Edge-Based Road Condition Monitoring for VANETs

Yan Xu[1,2,3], Meng Wang[1,2] (ID), Jie Cui[1,2], Jing Zhang[1,2],
and Hong Zhong[1,2(✉)] (ID)

[1] School of Computer Science and Technology, Anhui University, Hefei, China
{xuyan,cuijie,zhongh}@ahu.edu.cn
[2] Anhui Engineering Laboratory of IoT Security Technologies, Hefei, Anhui, China
[3] Shaanxi Key Laboratory of Information Communication Network and Security,
Xi'an University of Posts and Telecommunications, Xi'an, China

Abstract. Road conditions are the main factor affecting traffic safety, so it is necessary to monitor road conditions. In vehicular ad-hoc networks (VANETs), the trusted authority (TA) is allowed to monitor road conditions with the help of the vehicle on the road. However, the TA may receive too much road condition information since the same road condition has not been filtered out. In this paper, we propose a lightweight privacy-preserving edge-based road condition monitoring (LPE-RCM) scheme. To reduce the burden of the TA, we use edge nodes to filter out redundant road conditions. Besides, to encourage the vehicle to report road conditions actively, we adopt a privacy-aware reputation mechanism. Finally, the security proof and analysis show that LPE-RCM satisfies the security requirements of VANETs. The experimental results show that LPE-RCM is acceptable.

Keywords: VANETs · Privacy preserving · Authentication · Road condition monitoring

1 Introduction

In VANETs, vehicles with on-board units (OBUs) can collect the real-time road condition information, such as traffic congestion, traffic accidents, traffic obstacles, and road damage, and report to TA with the help of the roadside units (RSUs). After that, the TA take timely actions, such as traffic light adjustment, traffic accident rescue, and barrier removal [7]. Therefore, continuous monitoring of road conditions is essential.

Many conditional privacy-preserving authentication (CPPA) schemes for VANETs [2,4] protect the privacy of the vehicle and ensure the integrity of the road condition information and the legality of the information source through the use of anonymous identities. To achieve the confidentiality of road conditions, Liu et al. [6] designed a privacy-enhanced traffic monitoring scheme in

© Springer Nature Switzerland AG 2020
D. Yu et al. (Eds.): WASA 2020, LNCS 12385, pp. 78–86, 2020.
https://doi.org/10.1007/978-3-030-59019-2_9

VANETs. However, the scheme is not suitable for complex and changeable road conditions. And it is unrealistic for the TA to process and store all road conditions. It should filter out the same road conditions in advance. Wang et al. [9] used the technology of the equality test of ciphertexts [10] to filter the ciphertexts generated by the same road conditions without knowing the content of the ciphertexts. However, too much information is concentrated on the cloud for processing, requiring high computing costs. Therefore, we use multiple edge nodes to help the TA filter out redundant road conditions in parallel. For this reason, storage and computing resources of edge nodes are as close as possible to the vehicle.

Besides, to reduce spurious road condition information from sources while encouraging vehicles to actively report road conditions, the reputation mechanism becoming more and more popular in VANETs [3]. However, when rewarding a vehicle, the vehicle's identity must remain the same in the scheme [5], which threatens the privacy of the vehicle. In other words, after the vehicle's identity is hidden, how to return the reward to the target vehicle is a problem to be solved.

Hence, designing a filterable and low-cost road condition monitoring scheme that ensures security and privacy is both a goal and a challenge. Our contributions are summarized below.

- We propose a lightweight privacy-preserving edge-based road condition monitoring scheme for VANETs. We make full use of the geographical advantages of the edge nodes distribution. In addition to being the communication medium between the vehicle and TA, the edge node also helps the TA filter out redundant road conditions at a lower cost.
- We adopt a privacy-aware reputation mechanism to reduce spurious information from sources. Constantly updated anonymous identity is used to protect the identity privacy of contributors, and only vehicles with a good reputation can obtain new anonymous identities and report road conditions. Furthermore, we solve the problem that the vehicle must hold the same identity to get rewards.
- We provide security analysis for LPE-RCM and show that LPE-RCM can realize conditional privacy protection, message authentication, and confidentiality of road condition information. Finally, we analyze the performance of LPE-RCM, which has a low cost in terms of computation cost and communication cost.

The rest of this paper is organized as follows. Sections 2 and 3 provide background and specific scheme, respectively. Then, Sect. 4 gives the security/privacy analysis. Section 5 analysis computation cost and communication cost. Finally, the conclusion is given in Sect. 6.

2 Background

2.1 System Model

LPE-RCM comprises three entities (see Fig. 1). That is the TA, the RSUs, and the vehicle. The TA is a trusted third party and has powerful computing and

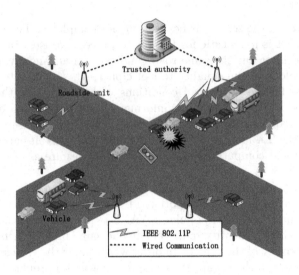

Fig. 1. System model

storage capabilities. It is responsible for initializing the system, delegating RSUs, and vehicles. The RSU is a wireless communication device, which can communicate vehicles with OBUs through the dedicated short-range communication protocol. The vehicle is equipped with an OBU. Once the vehicle detects terrible road conditions, it transmits them to the nearest RSU. The RSU as the edge node filters out redundant road conditions, and only sends the filtered ones to the TA.

2.2 Security Threats

Security threats may come from external and internal attackers. Global eavesdroppers can obtain information between entities by monitoring the open communication channel [8]. The internal attacker could be RSUs or vehicles. RSUs are semi-honest. Vehicles are also curious about the privacy of other vehicles. And some vehicles may be malicious. For example, they fake other legitimate vehicles to report untrue road conditions.

3 The Proposed LPE-RCM

3.1 System Setup

At this stage, the TA initializes the system.

- The TA selects two large prime numbers p, q, a non-singular elliptic curve $E : y^2 = x^3 + ax + b \ mod \ p$, and a generator P with the order q of a group G, which is made of all points on the E and the infinity O, where $a, b \in F_p$.

- The TA randomly selects $x, s \in Z_q^*$ and calculates $P_{pub} = x \cdot P$, where x is the private key, P_{pub} is the public key, and s is updated secret key.
- The TA selects secure hash functions $h_i : \{0,1\}^* \to Z_q$ ($1 \leq i \leq 12, i \in Z_q^*$).
- The TA sends system parameters $\{p, q, a, b, P, P_{pub}, h_1, h_2, \cdots, h_{12}\}$ to all RSUs and vehicles.

3.2   Delegation

At this stage, the TA registers RSUs and vehicles offline.

Delegation to RSUs. Each RSU gets a private key rsk from the TA.

- The TA generates a secret key $rsk = h_1(x || ID_{RSU})$ for the RSU with identity ID_{RSU} and sends rsk to the RSU secretly.
- The RSU calculates the public key $RPK = rsk \cdot P$ and broadcasts RPK to nearby vehicles regularly.

Delegation to Vehicles. Each vehicle gets an anonymous identity $AID_i = \{AID_{i,1}, AID_{i,2}\}$ and the corresponding private key osk_i from the TA.

- The user sends real identity RID to the TA secretly.
- The TA randomly selects $w_i \in Z_q^*$ and calculates $AID_{i,1} = w_i \cdot P$, $AID_{i,2} = RID \oplus h_2(x || AID_{i,1})$, and $osk_i = w_i + x \cdot h_3(AID_{i,1} || AID_{i,2}) \mod q$.
- The TA stores $\{s, RID, AID_i, osk_i\}$ into the vehicle's OBU_i and maintains a database $(RID, (X, Y))$, where (X, Y) represents the vehicle's reputation.

3.3   Road Condition Generation

At this stage, the OBU_i encrypts and signs road condition information $M_i \in \{0,1\}^*$, where M_i includes road conditions and road sections.

- The OBU_i calculates $P_1 = (h_4(M_i), h_5(M_i))$, $P_2 = (h_6(M_i), h_7(M_i))$, makes a straight line $f(x)$ with P_1 and P_2, and calculates $y_{i,1} = f(x_{i,1})$ and $y_{i,2} = f(x_{i,2})$, where $x_{i,1}, x_{i,2} \in Z_q^*$ are random numbers.
- The OBU_i randomly selects $s_i \in Z_q^*$, calculates $C_{i,1} = s_i \cdot P$, $C_{i,2} = M_i \oplus h_8(s_i \cdot P_{pub})$, $C_{i,3} = (x_{i,1} || x_{i,2} || y_{i,1} || y_{i,2}) \oplus h_9(s_i \cdot RPK, C_{i,1}, C_{i,2})$, and $\delta_i = osk_i + s_i \cdot h_{10}(AID_i || C_i || T_i) \mod q$, and sends $(AID_i, C_i, T_i, \delta_i)$ to the nearby RSU, where T_i is the current timestamp and $C_i = \{C_{i,1}, C_{i,2}, C_{i,3}\}$.

3.4   Road Condition Filtering

At this stage, redundant road conditions can be filtered out.

Reliability Verification. Upon receiving $(AID_i, C_i, T_i, \delta_i)$ from the OBU_i, the RSU performs the following steps.

- The RSU verifies the freshness of T_i. If it is not fresh, the RSU stops.
- The RSU checks whether $\delta_i \cdot P = AID_{i,1} + P_{pub} \cdot h_{i,3} + C_{i,1} \cdot h_{i,10}$ holds, where $h_{i,3} = h_{i,3}(AID_{i,1} \| AID_{i,2})$ and $h_{i,10} = h_{10}(AID_i \| C_i \| T_i)$. If it does not hold, the RSU ignores the road condition. Otherwise, the RSU considers the road condition reliable and go ahead.

Our scheme supports batch verification. Similarly, the RSU can check whether the equation $(\sum_{i=1}^{n} v_i \cdot \delta_i) \cdot P = \sum_{i=1}^{n}(v_i \cdot AID_{i,1}) + P_{pub} \cdot \sum_{i=1}^{n}(v_i \cdot h_{i,3}) + \sum_{i=1}^{n}(v_i \cdot C_{i,1} \cdot h_{i,10})$ $(1 \le i \le n)$ holds, where $v_i \in [1, 2^t]$ and t are small random integers.

Equality Test. If $(AID_i, C_i, T_i, \delta_i)$ from the OBU_i is reliable, the RSU sequentially compares it with each existing $(AID_j, C_j, T_i, \delta_i)$ in the RSU's local library.

- The RSU calculates $x_{i,1} \| x_{i,2} \| y_{i,1} \| y_{i,2} \leftarrow C_{i,3} \oplus h_9(rsk \cdot C_{i,1}, C_{i,1}, C_{i,2})$, $x_{j,1} \| x_{j,2} \| y_{j,1} \| y_{j,2} \leftarrow C_{j,3} \oplus h_9(rsk \cdot C_{j,1}, C_{j,1}, C_{j,2})$, $f_i(x) \leftarrow ((x_{i,1}, y_{i,1}), (x_{i,2}, y_{i,2}))$, and $f_j(x) \leftarrow ((x_{j,1}, y_{j,1}), (x_{j,2}, y_{j,2}))$. If $f_i(x) = f_j(x)$, the RSU considers that the road condition has been reported and stops.
- The RSU sends the tuple $(AID_i, C_i, T_i, \delta_i)$, ID_{RSU}, and the current timestamp T_j to the TA, and records $(AID_i, C_i, T_i, \delta_i)$ in the local library.

3.5 Road Condition Decryption

At this stage, the TA decrypts road conditions from the RSU.

- The TA verifies the freshness of T_j. If it is not fresh, the TA stops.
- The TA performs reliability verification like the RSU.
- The TA calculates $M_i \leftarrow C_{i,2} \oplus H_8(x \cdot C_{i,1}, C_{i,1}, C_{i,2})$, $rsk \leftarrow h_1(x \| ID_{RSU})$, and $x_{i,1} \| x_{i,2} \| y_{i,1} \| y_{i,2} \leftarrow C_{i,3} \oplus h_9(rsk \cdot C_{i,1}, C_{i,1}, C_{i,2})$.
- The TA constructs a straight line $f(x)$ with M_i like that in Road Condition Report and checks whether $y_{i,1} = f(x_{i,1})$ and $y_{i,2} = f(x_{i,2})$ are correct. If one of the two equations is incorrect, the TA stops. Otherwise, the TA accepts M_i.

3.6 Reputation Management

At this stage, the TA updates the OBU_i's reputation (X, Y).

The TA extracts the vehicle's real identity $RID \leftarrow AID_{i,2} \oplus h_2(x \| AID_{i,1})$ and gets (X, Y) from the database $(RID_j, (X, Y))$. If the vehicle does good, X increases. If the vehicle does bad, Y increases.

3.7 Anonymous-ID and Private Key Update

At this stage, the TA updates anonymous identity AID_i and the private key osk_i for the vehicle OBU_i whose reputation meets the criteria.

- The TA randomly selects $w_i' \in Z_q^*$ and calculates $AID_{i,1}' = w_i' \cdot P$, $AID_{i,2}' = RID \oplus h_2(x||AID_{i,1}')$, and $osk_i' = w_i' + x \cdot h_3(AID_{i,1}'||AID_{i,2}') \bmod q$.
- The TA calculates $\delta_{TA} = x + w_i' \cdot h_{12}(AID_i'||C_{osk_i}||T_{TA}) \bmod q$ and sends $\{AID_i', C_{osk_i}, T_{TA}, \delta_{TA}\}$ to the OBU_i, where T_{TA} is the current timestamp and $C_{osk_i} = osk_i' \oplus h_{11}(RID||s)$.
- The OBU_i verifies the freshness of T_{TA}, then verifies if the equation $\delta_{TA} \cdot P = AID_{i,1}' + h_{12}(AID_i'||C_{osk_i}||T_{TA}) \cdot P_{pub}$ holds. If it holds, the OBU_i gets $osk_i' \leftarrow C_{osk_i} \oplus h_{11}(RID||s)$ and accepts it. Otherwise, the OBU_i ignores it.

4 Security/Privacy Analysis

In this section, we show that LPE-RCM can achieve the following security/privacy preservation features.

- **Conditional Privacy Preservation**: The vehicle's real identity is unknown except for the TA. Using the system private key x, the TA can get $RID \leftarrow AID_{i,2} \oplus h_2(x||AID_{i,1})$. However, the adversary does not know x.
- **Message Authentication**: The RSU and the TA could verify that the source of the message is legitimate. And the TA can verify that the message reported by the vehicle is complete.
- **Privacy Preservation of Road Conditions**: The road condition information should be sent in the form of ciphertext to ensure that the information is not leaked.

5 Performance Analysis

In this section, we compare LPE-RCM with the road condition monitoring scheme [9] in terms of computation cost and communication cost.

Set the security level to 80 bits. For the scheme [9], a bilinear pairing $\bar{e} : G_1 \times G_1 \to G_2$ is used, where G_1 is an additive group generated by the generator $\bar{P}$ with the order $\bar{q}$ on the super singular elliptic curve $\bar{E} : y^2 = x^3 + x \bmod \bar{p}$, and $\bar{p}$ and $\bar{q}$ are 512-bit and 160-bit prime numbers, respectively. For the the elliptic curve cryptosystem (ECC)-based scheme (LPE-RCM), an additive group G is used, where G with the order q and generator P is made of all points on a non-singular elliptic curve $E : y^2 = x^3 + ax + b \bmod p$, where $a, b \in Z_p^*$, p and q are 160-bit prime numbers.

Table 1. Comparison of computation cost.

	Wang et al.'s scheme [9]	LPE-RCM
MES	$4T_{exp}^{bp} + 1T_{mtp} + 2T_h$	$3T_{sm}^{ecc} + 7T_h$
VOM	$3T_{exp}^{bp} + 2T_{bp} + 3T_h$	$3T_{sm}^{ecc} + 2T_{pa}^{ecc} + 2T_h$
ETOM	$2T_{bp}$	$2T_{sm}^{ecc} + 2T_h$
DVOM	$4T_{exp}^{bp} + 4T_{bp} + 1T_{mtp} + 4T_h$	$5T_{sm}^{bp} + 2T_{pa}^{ecc} + 9T_h$
VMM	$(3n)T_{exp}^{bp} + (2n)T_{bp} + (3n)T_h$	$(n+2)T_{sm}^{ecc} + (3n-1)T_{pa}^{ecc}$ $+ (2n)T_{sm-s}^{ecc} + (2n)T_h$
ETMM	$(2n)T_{bp}$	$(2n)T_{sm}^{ecc} + (2n)T_h$
DVMM	$(4n)T_{exp}^{bp} + (4n)T_{bp} + (n)T_{mtp} +$ $(4n)T_h$	$(3n+2)T_{sm}^{ecc} + (3n-1)T_{pa}^{ecc}$ $+ (2n)T_{sm-s}^{ecc} + (4n+1)T_h$

5.1   Computation Cost Analysis

In this subsection, we analyze the computation cost of LPE-RCM and Wang et al.'s scheme [9]. We use MIRACL [1] to compute the execution time of every stage. Our hardware platform includes an Intel $I7-6700$ processor, $8G$ memory, and runs windows 7 operating system. $\overline{P}, \overline{S}, \overline{T} \in G_1$, $P, S, T \in G$, $\overline{x} \in Z_q^*$, $x \in Z_q^*$, $a, v_i \in [1, 2^t]$, and a, t, v_i are small integers. The execution time of $\overline{P}^a$ is $T_{exp}^{bp} = 2.1456(t=5)$ ms. The execution time of $\overline{e}(\overline{S}, \overline{T})$ is $T_{bp} = 5.086$ ms. The execution time of $\overline{x} \cdot \overline{P}$ is $T_{sm}^{bp} = 0.694$ ms. The execution time of $\overline{S} + \overline{T}$ is $T_{pa}^{bp} = 0.0018$ ms. The execution time of the hash-to-point function is $T_{mtp}^{bp} = 0.0992$ ms. The execution time of $x \cdot P$ is $T_{sm}^{ecc} = 0.3218$ ms. The execution time of $v_i \cdot P$ is $T_{sm-s}^{ecc} = 0.0246(t=5)$ ms. The execution time of $S+T$ is $T_{pa}^{ecc} = 0.0024$ ms. The execution time of the hash function is $T_h = 0.001$ ms.

Let MES, VOM, ETOM, and DVOM denote one message encryption and signing, verification, equality test, and decryption and validation of a message, respectively. Furthermore, let VMM, ETMM, and DVMM denote verification, equality tests, and decryption and validation of multiple messages, respectively. The comparison of computation costs for each stage is shown in Table 1 and Fig. 2. LPE-RCM has lower computation costs in all stages.

5.2   Communication Cost Analysis

In this subsection, we analyze the communication costs of LPE-RCM and the scheme [9]. The sizes of the elements in G_1 and G are 128 and 40 bytes, respectively. And the sizes of the hash-to-point function's output, the hash function's output, and timestamp are 64, 20 and 4 bytes, respectively. In the scheme [9], the communication cost is $128 \times 5 + 64 \times 7 + 4 \times 3 = 1100$ bytes. In LPE-RCM, the communication cost is $40 \times 3 + 20 \times 4 + 4 = 204$ bytes. Therefore, LPE-RCM has a lower communication cost.

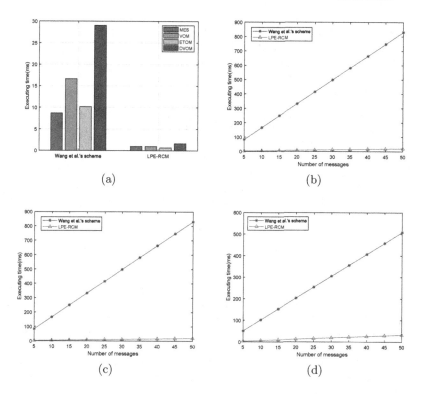

(a)

(b)

(c)

(d)

Fig. 2. The execution time of every stage. (a) Computational latency for a message. (b) Delay in batch verification for multiple messages. (c) Delay in equality tests for multiple messages. (d) Delay in decryption and validation for multiple messages.

6 Conclusion

In this paper, we design a lightweight privacy-preserving edge-based road condition monitoring scheme for VANETs. We make full use of the edge node to help the TA to filter out redundant road conditions. Besides, we adopt a privacy-aware reputation mechanism, and the change of the vehicle's anonymity identity does not affect the management of the vehicle's reputation. Only vehicles with a good reputation can obtain a new anonymous identity and report road conditions, so reducing spurious information from sources. Finally, we prove that LPE-RCM not only ensures the reliability and confidentiality of road condition information but also protects the privacy of the vehicle. Performance analysis shows that LPE-RCM has apparent advantages in computing and communication overhead.

Acknowledgements. The work was supported by the National Natural Science Foundation of China (Nos. 61702005, 61872001), the Open Fund of Shaanxi Key Laboratory of Information Communication Network and Security (Xi'an University of Posts &

Telecommunications), (No. ICNS201804). The authors are very grateful to the anonymous referees for their detailed comments and suggestions regarding this paper.

References

1. MIRACL Homepage. http://shamus.ie/?page=home. Accessed 4 Oct 2019
2. Cui, J., Zhang, J., Zhong, H., Xu, Y.: SPACF: a secure privacy-preserving authentication scheme for VANET with cuckoo filter. IEEE Trans. Veh. Technol. **66**(11), 10283–10295 (2017). https://doi.org/10.1109/TVT.2017.2718101
3. Cui, J., Zhang, X., Zhong, H., Ying, Z., Liu, L.: RSMA: reputation system-based lightweight message authentication framework and protocol for 5G-enabled vehicular networks. IEEE Internet Things J. **6**(4), 6417–6428 (2019). https://doi.org/10.1109/JIOT.2019.2895136
4. He, D., Zeadally, S., Xu, B., Huang, X.: An efficient identity-based conditional privacy-preserving authentication scheme for vehicular ad hoc networks. IEEE Trans. Inf. Forensics Secur. **10**(12), 2681–2691 (2015). https://doi.org/10.1109/TIFS.2015.2473820
5. Hussain, R., et al.: Secure and privacy-aware incentives-based witness service in social internet of vehicles clouds. IEEE Internet Things J. **5**(4), 2441–2448 (2018)
6. Liu, Y., Ling, J., Wu, Q., Qin, B.: Scalable privacy-enhanced traffic monitoring in vehicular ad hoc networks. Soft Comput. **20**(8), 3335–3346 (2015). https://doi.org/10.1007/s00500-015-1737-y
7. Mohseni-Ejiyeh, A., Ashouri-Talouki, M.: Sevr+ : secure and privacy-aware cloud-assisted video reporting service for 5G vehicular networks. In: Iranian Conference on Electrical Engineering (2017)
8. Ni, J., Zhang, K., Yu, Y., Lin, X., Shen, X.: Privacy-preserving smart parking navigation supporting efficient driving guidance retrieval. IEEE Trans. Veh. Technol. **67**(7), 6504–6517 (2018). https://doi.org/10.1109/TVT.2018.2805759
9. Wang, Y., Ding, Y., Wu, Q., Wei, Y., Qin, B., Wang, H.: Privacy-preserving cloud-based road condition monitoring with source authentication in VANETs. IEEE Trans. Inf. Forensics Secur. **14**(7), 1779–1790 (2019). https://doi.org/10.1109/TIFS.2018.2885277
10. Yang, G., Tan, C.H., Huang, Q., Wong, D.S.: Probabilistic public key encryption with equality test. In: Pieprzyk, J. (ed.) CT-RSA 2010. LNCS, vol. 5985, pp. 119–131. Springer, Heidelberg (2010). https://doi.org/10.1007/978-3-642-11925-5_9

Joint Switch Upgrade and VNF Placement for NFV-Based SDNs

Minli Zhang, Hongli Xu$^{(\boxtimes)}$, Xingpeng Fan, Da Yao, and Liusheng Huang

School of Computer Science and Technology,
University of Science and Technology of China, Hefei 230027, Anhui, China
{zml2018,fx364117,yddzf}@mail.ustc.edu.cn,
{xuhongli,lshuang}@ustc.edu.cn

Abstract. With the centralized control of SDN, operators can easily manage the network and flexibly forward flows to achieve certain objects for Network Functions Virtualization (NFV). Previous works focus on placing Virtual Network Functions (VNFs) in pure SDNs for network functions virtualization. Due to the heterogeneity of hybrid SDNs, the method of placing VNFs in pure SDNs may become infeasible in hybrid SDNs. Moreover, the existing solutions first evolve the traditional network to hybrid SDN and then place VNFs in the hybrid network. However, because of limited computing resources and flow table size, placing VNFs directly in a hybrid SDN network may require the deployment of more servers. To solve these problems, we propose to jointly consider switch upgrade and VNF placement to evolve the traditional network into a hybrid NFV-based SDN. At the beginning of upgrading legacy switches to SDN switches, VNFs are placed at the same time. We formalize the joint problem of switch upgrade and VNF placement (JSV), then prove it to be NP-hard. Then, a knapsack-based approximation algorithm is proposed to solve the JSV problem. Simulation results show that the algorithm can reduce the number of servers by about 20% compared with SDN-First algorithm and the number of maximum rules by about 50% compared with NFV-First algorithm.

Keywords: Software-Defined Network · Hybrid network · Network Function Virtualization · Virtual network function

1 Introduction

Software-Defined Network (SDN) and Network Functions Virtualization (NFV) are independent but complementary technologies, and combining them can give full play to their respective potentials [7]. On the one hand, SDN plays an important role in the orchestration of NFV infrastructure resources (including physical and virtual resources). On the other hand, SDN can also benefit from the core functions such as virtual infrastructure management and orchestration introduced by NFV. Therefore, the combination of SDN and NFV has attracted widespread attention from academia [7]. Previous works [9] study the placement

© Springer Nature Switzerland AG 2020
D. Yu et al. (Eds.): WASA 2020, LNCS 12385, pp. 87–95, 2020.
https://doi.org/10.1007/978-3-030-59019-2_10

of VNFs in pure SDNs to achieve network function virtualization. However, due to time and cost constraints, SDN is usually deployed in an incremental strategy. For example, AT&T upgraded 55% of its network to SDN at the end of 2017 and planed to convert 75% of its network to SDN by 2020 [4]. Therefore, for a long time, legacy switches will coexist with SDN switches, and VNFs needs to be placed in a hybrid SDN network for network function virtualization. At the same time, previous works [4,10] to evolve the traditional network to SDN did not consider the CPU resources and flow table size required to place the VNF. Placing VNFs on such a hybrid SDN may require the deployment of more servers.

To solve the above challenges, we propose to jointly consider switch upgrade and VNF placement to evolve the traditional network into a hybrid NFV-based SDN. The main contributions of this paper are summarized as follows:

- We formalize the JSV problem, which is designed to minimize the cost of evolving a traditional network into a hybrid NFV-based SDN, subject to the flow table size constraint of each SDN switch and the computing resource constraint of each server.
- We propose a knapsack-based approximation algorithm with provable approximate ratios.
- We evaluate the performance of the proposed algorithm through simulations. The simulation results show that the comprehensive performance of our proposed algorithm is better than the existing solutions.

2 Preliminaries and Problem Formulation

2.1 Network and Flow Models

A traditional network typically consists of a set of legacy switches, $V = \{v_1, ..., v_n\}$, with $n = |V|$. Thus, the network topology can be modeled by $G = (V, E)$, where E is the set of links connecting switches. We denote the flows based on originator-destination (OD) pairs as $\Gamma = \{\gamma_1, ..., \gamma_m\}$, with m = $|\Gamma|$. The intensity of the flow γ represented by $c(\gamma)$. We use Γ_v to denote the set of flows through switch $v \in V$. In this network, we assume that each device runs a traditional IP routing protocol, such as OSPF, and each device follows the shortest path to the destination [10]. The set of shortest path switches for flow γ is V_γ.

A set of virtual network functions, e.g., IDS, DPI, Firewall, is denoted as $\mathcal{F} = \{f_1, ..., f_q\}$, with $q = |\mathcal{F}|$. For simplicity, we assume that each VNF can work independently from other VNFs. Each VNF $f \in \mathcal{F}$ is associated with a unit processing cost, denoted as $\theta(f)$. Since we do not consider the VNF processing order in the server deployment, the VNF requirements set of flow γ is denoted as $\mathcal{F}_\gamma$. If $F_\gamma \neq \emptyset$, we construct a virtual request r_γ^f for flow γ and each VNF $f \in \mathcal{F}_\gamma$. Note that not all flows in the network can construct virtual requests. The virtual request set $\mathcal{R}_v^f$ denotes the set of virtual requests that need to be processed by VNF f in switch v. i.e., $\mathcal{R}_v^f = \{r_\gamma^f | \gamma \in \Gamma_v, f \in \mathcal{F}_\gamma\}$. If virtual requests $r_\gamma^f \in \mathcal{R}_v^f$ is processed by VNF $f \in \mathcal{F}$, the processing cost for this flow is $\theta(f) \cdot c(\gamma)$. When several instants of different VNFs are placed on a server, the total processing cost does not exceed the server's CPU computing resource capacity. The CPU processing capacity of the server s_v deployed on the switch v is $C(v)$. If a flow passes through an SDN switch, it is a programmable flow and we can take advantage of SDN by flexible routing. If the virtual request r_γ^f is processed on a server, it is a covered virtual request.

2.2   Relationship Between Server Placement and SDN Switch

In our question, we require that the server must be deployed on the SDN switch in the upgraded network. We have two main considerations. On the one hand, with the centralized control of SDN, operators can easily and flexibly manage the NFV network, and can achieve some goals of managing traffic through flexible routing [11]. Deploying servers on legacy switches cannot enjoy the benefits of SDN. On the other hand, many enterprises (e.g., China Telecom, VMware, and Huawei) adopt the SDN overlay solution to deploy SDN networks [2]. Servers deployed on SDN switches are visible to the overlay network, while servers deployed on legacy switches are not necessarily visible to the overlay network.

It is worth noting that the deployment of servers on SDN switches brings new constraints, such as flow table size (FTS). SDN switches use Ternary Content Addressable Memory (TCAM) to store flow table entries. Compared with RAM-based storage on switches, TCAM is more expensive and consumes more power per Mbit [6]. In order not to affect the normal forwarding of the switch, the entries consumed by the VNF placement should only occupy a part of the TCAM storage space. So it is very important to choose the right switches node for upgrading and placing the VNFs.

2.3   Problem Formulation

In this section, we give the definition of the JSV problem. We use $x_v \in \{0, 1\}$ to denote whether switch v is upgraded to the SDN switch. Similarly, we use $y_v \in \{0, 1\}$ to denote whether a server is deployed on v. The switch of the deployed server must be a switch that has been upgraded to SDN. For simplicity, in our problem, only one server will be deployed on an SDN switch. Let $z_{v,f}^\gamma \in \{0, 1\}$ denote whether virtual request r_γ^f is covered by the server deployed on switch v.

Accordingly, we formulate the JSV problem as follows:

$$\min \quad \sum_{v \in V} (x_v + \lambda \cdot y_v)$$

$$
\text{S.t.} \begin{cases}
x_v \geq y_v, & \forall v \in V \\
y_v \geq z_{v,f}^{\gamma}, & \forall v \in V, \gamma \in \Gamma_v, f \in \mathcal{F}_{\gamma} \\
\sum_{\gamma \in \Gamma_v} \sum_{f \in \mathcal{F}_{\gamma}} \theta(f) \cdot z_{v,f}^{\gamma} \cdot c(\gamma) \leq C(v), & \forall v \in V \\
\sum_{\gamma \in \Gamma_v} \sum_{f \in \mathcal{F}_{\gamma}} z_{v,f}^{\gamma} \leq M(v), & \forall v \in V \\
\sum_{v \in V_{\gamma}} x_v \geq 1, & \forall \gamma \in \Gamma \\
\sum_{v \in V_{\gamma}} z_{v,f}^{\gamma} = 1, & \forall \gamma \in \Gamma, f \in \mathcal{F}_{\gamma} \\
x_v, y_v, z_{v,f}^{\gamma} \in \{0,1\}, & \forall v \in V, \gamma \in \Gamma, f \in \mathcal{F}_{\gamma}
\end{cases} \tag{1}
$$

The first set of inequalities denotes that the server must be deployed on an SDN switch. The second set of inequalities denotes that VNFs must be deployed on the server. The third set of inequalities denotes that the total processing cost of VNFs should not exceed the computing resource capacity of the server. The fourth set of inequalities denotes that flow table size constraint and each processing a virtual request consumes a flow table entry. The fifth set of inequalities denotes that each flow must pass through at least one SDN switch in order to be programmed. The sixth set of equations denotes that all virtual requests must be covered. Assuming that the cost of a server is λ times that of an SDN switch, our optimization objective is to minimize the cost of upgrading to the hybrid NFV-based SDN.

Theorem 1. *The JSV problem is NP-hard.*

Proof. The proof of Theorem 1 is omitted because of space limitation.

3   Algorithm Design

In this section, we propose a knapsack-based approximation algorithm for JSV problem and give the performance analysis.

3.1   A Knapsack-Based Algorithm for JSV

In this section, we propose an approximate algorithm called KSV to solve the JSV problem. Before describing the algorithm, we first consider a 0–1 knapsack problem [12], which is to place VNFs on the switch to cover as many virtual requests as possible. The capacity of the knapsack considers both the computing resource capacity of the server and the flow table size of the switch.

We first take a greedy algorithm called KP to solve the 0–1 knapsack problem. Previous work [5] has proved that the KP algorithm has an approximate ratio of 2 to the 0–1 knapsack problem. We use P to denote the set of selected VNFs on a switch. The profit value α_v^f denotes the number of virtual requests that can be covered by VNF f placed on switch v. Moreover, we use α_v^f and β_v^f to denote the rule cost and CPU resource cost of the virtual requests covered by the VNF f on switch v, respectively. For the convenience of calculation, we use σ_v^f to denote the comprehensive cost of the two types of costs. In the KP algorithm, we calculate the profit of each unselected VNF f and its corresponding rule cost and CPU capacity cost. Then, we rank all unselected VNFs in descending order

Algorithm 1. KP Algorithm on Switch v

1: $F \leftarrow \mathcal{F}, P \leftarrow \phi$
2: $\widetilde{C}(v) \leftarrow C(v), \widetilde{M}(v) \leftarrow M(v)$
3: **for** each VNF $f \in F$ **do**
4:     $\alpha_v^f = |\mathcal{R}_v^f|$
5:     $\beta_v^f = c(\mathcal{R}_v^f) \cdot \theta(f)$
6:     $\sigma_v^f = (\alpha_v^f, \beta_v^f)$
7: Rank the VNFs $f \in F$ in the decreasing order with the unit profit $\frac{\alpha_v^f}{|\sigma_v^f|}$.
8: **while** $\alpha_v^f \leq \widetilde{M}(v)$ *and* $\beta_v^f \leq \widetilde{C}(v)$ **do**
9:     $P = P \cup f$
10:    $\widetilde{C}(v) = \widetilde{C}(v) - \beta_v^f$
11:    $\widetilde{M}(v) = \widetilde{M}(v) - \alpha_v^f$
12:    $F = F - \{f\}$
13: **for** each unselected VNF $f \in F$ **do**
14:    **if** $\sum_{t \in P} c(\mathcal{R}_v^t) \leq c(\mathcal{R}_v^f)$ **then**
15:        $P \leftarrow \{f\}$
16: **return** P

of unit profit. Under the constraints of CPU capacity and flow table size, KP algorithm greedily selects VNF with the maximum profit per unit to join P. The KP algorithm is described in Algorithm 1.

We then propose the KSV algorithm for JSV. In the JSV problem, each flow needs to be programmable and each virtual request needs to be covered. Let $\widetilde{V}$ denote the set of selected switches that need to be upgraded. Let $\widetilde{S}$ denote the set of deployment servers. Let R_v denote the set of virtual requests KSV algorithm chooses to process on switch v, and we can place VNFs on switch v according to R_v. Moreover, We use $\widetilde{\Gamma}_v$ to represent the set of non-programmable flows in switch v, and $\widetilde{R}_f$ to represents the set of virtual requests not covered by VNF $f \in \mathcal{F}$. $\widetilde{R}_v^f$ represents the set of virtual requests that are not covered by VNF f in switch v.

The KSV algorithm is divided into two steps. The first step consists of a set of iterations. Each iteration of the KSV algorithm will select a switch to upgrade to SDN and deploy a server on it. In the first step, the KSV algorithm takes the KP algorithm to obtain a set of selected VNFs for each switch $v \in V - \widetilde{V}$. Then KSV calculate the virtual requests profit $\sum_{f \in P_v} |\widetilde{R}_v^f|$. The KSV algorithm choose the switch v with the maximum profit to upgrade to SDN and deploy the server. At the same time, the VNFs selected by the KP algorithm will also be placed on the server. Next, the KSV algorithm will update the set of non-programmable flows and the set of uncovered virtual requests. The first step will terminate until each virtual request has been covered. The second step also consists of a set of iterations. Each iteration selects the switch v with the maximum number of non-programmable flows to upgrade to SDN. The algorithm will terminate until all flows can be programmed. The KSV algorithm is formally described in Algorithm 2.

Algorithm 2. KSV: Knapsack-based Algorithm for JSV

1: $\widetilde{V} \leftarrow \phi; \widetilde{S} \leftarrow \phi; R_v \leftarrow \phi, \forall v \in V$

2: $\widetilde{\Gamma} \leftarrow \Gamma; \widetilde{\mathcal{R}}_f \leftarrow \mathcal{R}_f, \forall f \in \mathcal{F}$

3: $\widetilde{\Gamma}_v \leftarrow \Gamma_v, \forall v \in V; \widetilde{\mathcal{R}}_v^f \leftarrow \mathcal{R}_v^f, \forall v \in V$ and $f \in \mathcal{F}$

4: **Step 1: Select switches to upgrade to SDN switches and deployment servers**

5: **while** $\widetilde{\mathcal{R}}_f \neq \phi, \forall f \in \mathcal{F}$ **do**

6:     **for** each $v \in V - \widetilde{V}$ **do**

7:         Select the set of VNFs $f \in \mathcal{F}$ according to the KP algorithm, $P_v \leftarrow KP(v)$.

8:         Select a switch v with the maximum profit $\sum_{f \in P_v} |\widetilde{\mathcal{R}}_v^f|$ and deploy a server.

9:     $\widetilde{V} = \widetilde{V} \cup \{v\}, \widetilde{S} = \widetilde{S} \cup \{v\}, \widetilde{\Gamma} = \widetilde{\Gamma} - \widetilde{\Gamma}_v$

10:     **for** each switch $t \in V - \widetilde{V}$ **do**

11:         $\widetilde{\Gamma}_t = \widetilde{\Gamma}_t - \widetilde{\Gamma}_v$

12:     **for** each VNF $f \in P_v$ **do**

13:         $\widetilde{\mathcal{R}}_f = \widetilde{\mathcal{R}}_f - \widetilde{\mathcal{R}}_v^f, \ R_v = R_v \cup \widetilde{\mathcal{R}}_v^f$

14:         **for** each switch $t \in V - \widetilde{S}$ **do**

15:             $\widetilde{\mathcal{R}}_t^f = \widetilde{\mathcal{R}}_t^f - \widetilde{\mathcal{R}}_v^f$

16: **Step 2: Upgrade the switch to make all flows programmed**

17: **while** $\widetilde{\Gamma} \neq \phi$ **do**

18:     **for** each $v \in \widetilde{V}$ **do**

19:         Select the switch with the maximum number of non-programmable flows according to the $|\Gamma_v|$

20:     $\widetilde{V} = \widetilde{V} \cup \{v\}, \widetilde{\Gamma} = \widetilde{\Gamma} - \widetilde{\Gamma}_v$

21:     **for** each switch $t \in V - \widetilde{V}$ **do**

22:         $\widetilde{\Gamma}_t = \widetilde{\Gamma}_t - \widetilde{\Gamma}_v$

23: **return** $\widetilde{V}; \widetilde{S}; R_v, \forall v \in V$

3.2   Performance Analysis for KSV

Theorem 2. *For the JSV problem, the KSV algorithm can achieve* $2 \cdot H(p \cdot q)$*-approximation for the number of deployed servers, where p and q represent the number of VNF types and the maximum number of virtual requests through switches.*

Theorem 3. *The KSV algorithm can achieve* $3 \cdot H(p \cdot q)$*-approximation for the number of deployed switches.*

Proof. The proofs of Theorem 2 and Theorem 3 is omitted because of space limitation.

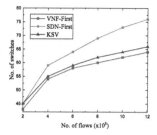

Fig. 1. No. of Switches vs. No. of flows.

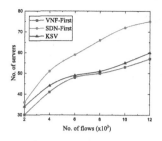

Fig. 2. No. of Servers vs. No. of flows.

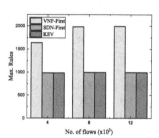

Fig. 3. Max. Rules vs. No. of flows.

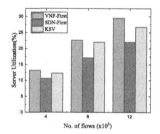

Fig. 4. Server Utilization vs. No. of flows.

4 Performance Evaluation

4.1 Simulation Settings and Benchmarks

In the simulation, we chose the Monash campus network topology [1] as the running example, which contains 100 switches and 200 hosts. Campus network is one of the typical application scenarios of SDN. We randomly select the originators and destinations address to generate flows, and randomly select some flows to generate the virtual requests. For the flow size, the 20% of the elephant flows may account for more than 80% of the total traffic [3]. We place five types of VNFs in the network, which is Load-Balancer, Firewall, NAT, IDS, Monitor, and their computing demands are adopted from [8]. The total CPU resource capacity of each server is set to 3 GHz. The flow table size provided by each SDN switch for processing VNFs is set to 1000.

In order to verify the performance of the KSV algorithm, we compared it with the other two state-of-the-art solutions. The first algorithm is SDN-First, which will first upgrade the switch to SDN, and then place VNFs on the SDN switch. If the SDN switch resources are insufficient to place all VNFs, it will greedily choose other switches to upgrade to SDN and deploy servers and VNFs. The second algorithm is VNF-First, which places VNF first and then upgrades the switch to SDN. Both benchmarks need to enable all flows to be programmed and all virtual requests to be covered.

4.2   Simulation Results

We mainly run four sets of simulations on Monash campus network topology to verify the performance of our proposed algorithm for the JSV problem. The first set of simulations compares the number of deployed switches by changing the number of flows 2 K to 12K. Figure 1 shows that the number of switches deployed by KSV is close to VNF-First, but less than SDN-First. For example, when the network 12 K flows, the number of switches that KSV needs to upgrade is about 15% less than SDN-First and about 5% more than VNF-First.

The second set of simulations compares the number of deployed servers by changing the number of flows 2 K to 12 K. Figure 2 shows that the number of server deployed by KSV is close to VNF-First, but less than SDN-First. For example, when the network 12 K flows, the KSV algorithm can reduce the number of deployed servers by approximately 20% compared to the VNF-First algorithm, while the KSV algorithm increases the number of deployed servers by only about 5% compared to VNF-First.

The third set of simulations compares the maximum flow table size consumption of the three algorithms by changing the number of flows 4 K to 12 K. Figure 3 shows that the maximum number of rules required by the VNF-First algorithm is more than KSV and SDN-First, which is also the reason why the number of VNF-First upgraded switches and the number of deployed servers are less than other algorithms. For example, when the network 12 K flows, the KSV algorithm can reduce the maximum number of rules by approximately 50% compared to the VNF-First.

The fourth set of simulations compares the average server utilization of the three algorithms by changing the number of flows 4 K to 12 K. Figure 4 shows that the average server utilization of KSV is close to VNF-First, but less than SDN-First. For example, the average server utilization rate of the KSV algorithm when the network 12 K flows is about 21% higher than SDN-First and about 9% lower than VNF-First.

Through the above simulation results, we can get the following conclusions. First, compared with the SDN-First algorithm, the KSV algorithm requires a smaller number of switches to be upgraded and a smaller number of servers to be deployed, and the server utilization rate of the KSV algorithm is higher. Second, compared with the VNF-First algorithm, the KSV algorithm can reduce the maximum number of rules by approximately 50%, and only need to pay an additional cost of about 5% to 9%.

5   Conclusion

In this paper, we propose the problem of joint switch upgrade and VNFs placement for hybrid NFV-based SDNs. We formalize the JSV problem and prove that it is NP-hard. A backpack-based algorithm is proposed to solve the JSV problem. The simulation results show that our proposed algorithm has high efficiency.

References

1. The network topology from the monash university (2017). http://www.ecse.mo nash.edu.au/twiki/bin/view/InFocus/LargePacket-switchingNetworkTopologies
2. Amin, R., Reisslein, M., Shah, N.: Hybrid SDN networks: a survey of existing approaches. IEEE Commun. Surv. Tutor. **20**(4), 3259–3306 (2018)
3. Curtis, A.R., Mogul, J.C., Tourrilhes, J., Yalagandula, P., Sharma, P., Banerjee, S.: DevoFlow: scaling flow management for high-performance networks. In: Proceedings of the ACM SIGCOMM 2011 Conference, pp. 254–265 (2011)
4. Guo, Z., Chen, W., Liu, Y.F., Xu, Y., Zhang, Z.L.: Joint switch upgrade and controller deployment in hybrid software-defined networks. IEEE J. Sel. Areas Commun. **37**(5), 1012–1028 (2019)
5. Gupta, A., Pál, M., Ravi, R., Sinha, A.: What about wednesday? approximation algorithms for multistage stochastic optimization. In: Chekuri, C., Jansen, K., Rolim, J.D.P., Trevisan, L. (eds.) Approximation, Randomization and Combinatorial Optimization. Algorithms and Techniques. APPROX 2005, RANDOM 2005. LNCS, vol. 3624, pp. 86–98. Springer, Berlin (2005). https://doi.org/10.1007/11538462_8
6. Katta, N., Alipourfard, O., Rexford, J., Walker, D.: Infinite CacheFow in software-defined networks. In: Proceedings of the Third Workshop on Hot Topics in Software Defined Networking, pp. 175–180 (2014)
7. Li, Y., Chen, M.: Software-defined network function virtualization: a survey. IEEE Access **3**, 2542–2553 (2015)
8. Martins, J., et al.: ClickOS and the art of network function virtualization. In: 11th USENIX Symposium on Networked Systems Design and Implementation (NSDI 2014), pp. 459–473 (2014)
9. Pei, J., Hong, P., Pan, M., Liu, J., Zhou, J.: Optimal VNF placement via deep reinforcement learning in SDN/NFV-enabled networks. IEEE J. Sel. Areas Commun. **38**(2), 263–278 (2019)
10. Poularakis, K., Iosifidis, G., Smaragdakis, G., Tassiulas, L.: One step at a time: optimizing SDN upgrades in ISP networks. In: IEEE INFOCOM 2017-IEEE Conference on Computer Communications, pp. 1–9. IEEE (2017)
11. Qazi, Z.A., Tu, C.C., Chiang, L., Miao, R., Sekar, V., Yu, M.: SIMPLE-fying middlebox policy enforcement using SDN. In: Proceedings of the ACM SIGCOMM 2013 Conference on SIGCOMM, pp. 27–38 (2013)
12. Shih, W.: A branch and bound method for the multiconstraint zero-one knapsack problem. J. Oper. Res. Soc. **30**(4), 369–378 (1979)

The Throughput Optimization
for Multi-hop MIMO Networks Based
on Joint IA and SIC

Peng Zhang[1,2], Xu Ding[1,2], Jing Wang[1,2], Zengwei Lyu[1], and Lei Shi[1(✉)]

[1] School of Computer Science and Information Engineering,
Hefei University of Technology, Hefei, China
`shilei@hfut.edu.cn`
[2] Institute of Industry and Equipment Technology, Hefei University of Technology,
Hefei, China

Abstract. MIMO researches penetrate the network community due to recent advances in MIMO degree-of-freedom (DoF) frameworks. Independent from MIMO, Successive Interference Cancellation (SIC) is a powerful multi-user detection technology in physical layer, and Interference Alignment (IA) is a powerful technique for handling interference. Based on the understanding of the strengths and weaknesses of SIC and DoF, we propose mutual assistance by joint IA, SIC and DoF-based Interference Cancellation (DoF IC) to (i) conserve precious DoF resources through IA and SIC; (ii) meet strict SINR threshold criteria through IC and IA. In this paper, we develop the mathematical model to achieve the two ideas in a multi-hop MIMO network. Combined with scheduling and routing constraints, we developed a cross-layer optimization framework to the throughput maximization problem with joint IA and SIC for MIMO networks. Simulation results show that the join of IA and SIC can significantly conserve DoFs for IC and thereby improve the throughput.

Keywords: IA · SIC · DoF · IC · MIMO · Multi-hop

1 Introduction

MIMO has been extensively researched and applied, due to its ability of spatial multiplexing (SM) gain and interference cancellation (IC) [1,2]. The concept of degree-of-freedom (DoF) was originally defined to represent the multiplexing gain of a MIMO channel. Now, the concept of DoF was extended to characterize nodes spatial freedom provided by its multiple antennas, and the basic idea of the DoF model is assigning DoF resources for SM or IC to nodes. Thus, DoFs are precious resources. Especially, when IC is used, it will reduce the remaining

Supported by National Natural Science Foundation of China with grant number[61701162] and the Fundamental Research Funds for the Central Universities with grant number [JZ2020HGQB0222, JZ2020HGQA0158].

D. Yu et al. (Eds.): WASA 2020, LNCS 12385, pp. 96–104, 2020.
https://doi.org/10.1007/978-3-030-59019-2_11

DoFs for SM. Hence, it is necessary to reduce the consumption of DoFs for IC, so that maximizes the available number of DoFs for SM.

Interference Alignment (IA) [4] offers a new direction to handle mutual interference among multi-user. The basic idea is to construct signals at transmitters so that these interference signals overlap at their unintended receivers. For multi-hop networks, IA is not advanced enough, since the interference models are much more complicated. Zeng et al. [3] studied OFDM-based IA in multi-hop cellular networks, but their work were limited to single-antenna networks. Li et al. [4] made the first attempt to explore IA in a multi-hop MIMO network, but the basic idea of IA (constructing signals) was not involved into their formulation.

SIC is a powerful multi-user detection technique used in physical layer [5,6]. Independent from MIMO, the receiver can iteratively decode out the required signals from multiple signals though using SIC [7]. The strongest signal can be decoded successfully, if it meets the SINR threshold. Research on exploiting SIC for nodes with single-antenna in a wireless network can be found in [8]. However, SIC does have its limitation that as long as one of the steps of the SINR can not be met, the subsequent procedures cannot be continued.

The main contributions of this paper are as follows:

- We develop an IM model with joint IA and SIC for multi-hop MIMO networks. We show that DoFs can be conserved if it satisfies the constraints in our IM model. Our model consists of (i) constraints at transmitters to determine the subset of interference streams for IA and (ii) constraints at receivers to determine the IA and SIC pattern of the interference streams.
- In multi-hop MIMO networks, coupling of both routing and scheduling with IM and DoF allocation is a nontrivial issue. We propose a scheme that addresses the flow routing and scheduling problem. On the one hand, IA and DoF IC can eliminate the barrier signals for SIC. On the other hand, DoF resources can be conserved through joint SIC and IA. Based on this scheme, the throughput will significantly increase in the multi-hop MIMO network.

2   The Background and Motivation

2.1   The Principles of the Three Technologies

Consider a MIMO network consisting of a set of nodes $\mathcal{N}$ with $N = |\mathcal{N}|$. Assume that each node have M antennas, and there are L possible links in the network. Denote $Tx(l)$ and $Rx(l)$ as the transmit and receive nodes of link l. We consider a time-slotted scheduling strategy, where a time frame consists of T time slots.

The number of DoFs represents the total available resources that can be used for SM and IC. SM refers to use DoFs for data streams transmission and reception, with each DoF being responsible for one data stream. IC refers to use DoFs to cancel interference, with each DoF corresponding to one interfering stream. IC can be used either at a transmitter or a receiver. For example, like the two links in Fig. 1(a), both nodes T_1 and R_1 consume z_1 DoFs for SM to

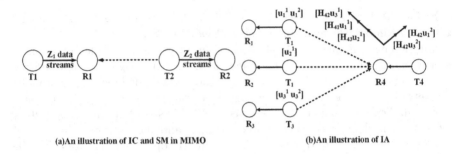

(a)An illustration of IC and SM in MIMO   (b)An illustration of IA

Fig. 1. The illustration of IC, SM and IA.

transmit z_1 data streams. For IC, if R_1 cancels this interference, it needs to consume z_2 DoFs. Or if T_2 cancels this interference, it needs z_1 DoFs.

IA refers to a construction of data streams at transmitters so that they align at the unintended receivers and remain resolvable at the intended receivers. Since the interfering streams are overlapped at a receiver, it can use fewer DoFs to cancel these interfering streams. As a result, the DoF resources will be conserved and used to transfer data. As shown in Fig. 1(b), without IA, R_4 needs to consume 5 DoFs to cancel the interference signals for IC. However, with IA, the 5 interfering can be aligned streams into 2 dimensions.

SIC allows a receiver to take multiple signals from different transmitters and decode each of them iteratively. For the composite received signal, the receiver attempts to iteratively decode the strongest signal and considers all other signals as noise. The process continues until all intended signals are successfully decoded, or the SINR threshold cannot be met at a certain stage.

2.2   Motivation and Basic Idea

After discussing the background, we find that the three technologies can help each other. *(i) DoF IC to remove barrier signal in SIC.* SIC will fail to continue, if the SINR threshold is no longer satisfied at any stage. Fortunately, we could use one DoF to cancel a particular interference for IC. After removing this signal, SIC can decode the remaining signals in the aggregate signal. *(ii) IA and SIC to conserve DoFs in IC.* Before we expend precious DoFs for IC, we exploit SIC and IA to its fullest extent at the receiver.

3   A Joint Design for Multi-hop MIMO Networks

We assume that a node cannot transmit or receive in one time slot. Denote $x_i[t]$ as a binary variable to indicate whether node i is a transmitter in time slot t, i.e., $x_i[t] = 1$ if node i is a transmitter in time slot t and 0 otherwise. Similarly, denote $y_i[t]$ as a binary variable to indicate whether node i is a receiver in time slot t. Then the half duplex constraints can be written as:

$$x_i[t] + y_i[t] \leq 1, (i \in \mathcal{N}, 1 \leq t \leq T). \tag{1}$$

Denote $z_l[t]$ as the number of data streams on link l in time slot t. If node i is a transmitter, we have $1 \le \sum_{l \in \mathcal{L}_i^{out}} z_l[t] \le M$, otherwise $\sum_{l \in \mathcal{L}_i^{out}} z_l[t] = 0$. Combining the two cases, the node activity constraints as follows:

$$x_i[t] \le \sum_{l \in \mathcal{L}_i^{out}} z_l[t] \le N_A \cdot x_i[t], (i \in \mathcal{N}, 1 \le t \le T), \tag{2}$$

$$y_i[t] \le \sum_{l \in \mathcal{L}_i^{in}} z_l[t] \le N_A \cdot y_i[t], (i \in \mathcal{N}, 1 \le t \le T). \tag{3}$$

3.1 IA in MIMO

Denote $\mathcal{A}_{ij}$ as the set of interfering streams from node i to node j, with $\alpha_{ij} = |\mathcal{A}_{ij}|$. Denote $\mathcal{B}_{ij}$ as the subset of interfering streams that are aligned to the other interfering streams at receiver j, with $\beta_{ij} = |\mathcal{B}_{ij}|$. For node i, $\mathcal{B}_{ij} \subseteq \mathcal{A}_{ij}$, e.g., $\beta_{ij}[t] \le \alpha_{ij}[t]$, where $\mathcal{I}_i$ is the set of nodes within the interfering range of i.

Each data stream corresponds to one precoding vector. Since each outgoing stream interferes with all the unintended receivers within the interference range of node i, the corresponding precoding vector determines the direction of one interfering stream for those receivers. For instance, precoding vector u_i^1 determines the directions of the outgoing stream at k receivers, only one of which is the intended receiver. Among the $k-1$ interfering streams, only one of them can be aligned to a particular direction by u_i^1. Since there are $\sum_{l \in L_i^{out}} z_l[t]$ precoding vectors at transmitter i, at most $\sum_{l \in L_i^{out}} z_l[t]$ interfering streams can be utilized by IA at their receivers. Then, we have: $\sum_{j \in \mathcal{I}_i} \beta_{ij}[t] \le \sum_{j \in \mathcal{L}_i^{out}} z_l[t]$.

For receiver i, there are three constraints that must be satisfied: (i) the interfering streams in each $\mathcal{B}_{ij}$ should not occupy independent directions at receiver j, so $\mathcal{B}_{ij}$ can only aligned to an interfering stream in $\cup_{i \in \mathcal{I}_j}(\mathcal{A}_{ij} \backslash \mathcal{B}_{ij})$; (ii) for resolvability, any interfering stream in $\mathcal{B}_{ij}$ and $\mathcal{A}_{ij}$ are linearly independent; (iii) any two interfering streams in $\mathcal{B}_{ij}$ cannot be aligned to the same interfering stream. The above conditions are all satisfied if the following constraint is satisfied: $\beta_{ij}[t] \le \sum_{k \in I_j}^{k \ne i}(\alpha_{kj}[t] - \beta_{kj}[t])$.

Since the DoFs consumed for SM and IC cannot exceed its total DoFs, we have the following constraint: $\sum_{l \in L_i^{in}} z_l[t] + \sum_{j \in \mathcal{I}_i}(\alpha_{ji}[t] - \beta_{ji}[t]) \le N_A \cdot y_i(t)$.

If node i is a transmitter and node j is a receiver in time slot t, we get $\alpha_{ij}[t] = \sum_{l \in L_i^{out}}^{R_X(l) \ne j} z_l[t]$, and 0 otherwise. Thus, we have:

$$\alpha_{ji}[t] = y_i[t] \cdot \sum_{l \in L_j^{out}}^{R_X(l) \ne i} z_l[t], (i \in \mathcal{I}_j, 1 \le j \le N, 1 \le t \le T). \tag{4}$$

3.2 SIC in MIMO

Consider the MIMO model, we assume that nodes are symbol synchronous and they may transmit up to M data streams. Depending on the transmit precoding vectors and receiver matrices, SINR can be calculated [9]. Assume data streams are uncorrelated, SINR for the qth element in y_{ji} is: $SINR_{ji}^q = \dfrac{p_j \cdot L_{ji}^2 \left\| (v_{ji}^q)' H_{ji}' u_j^q \right\|^2}{\sum_{k \in I_i, k \neq j} p_k L_{ki}^2 \left\| (v_{ji}^q)' H_{ki}' U_k \right\|^2 + N_0}$, where N_0 is equal to $N_0 \left\| v_{ji}^q \right\|^2$, due to $\left\| v_{ji}^q \right\|^2 = 1$; L_{ji} is the path-loss factor between node j and i; H_{ji} is the channel matrix between node j and i and is normalized to mean power 1, u_{ji}^q and v_j^q define as the precoding vector and the decoding vector, respectively.

For MIMO, there are usually multiple data streams from a transmitter, so we use the worst-case aggregate SINR for the same transmitter. If the worst-case data stream from node j is decodable, all data streams from node j can be decoded. For generality, suppose that the minimum received power levels of the data streams from the q transmitters at node i are listed in non-decreasing order as $p_q L_{qi}^2 C_{qi} \geq \cdots \geq p_n L_{ni}^2 \geq \cdots \geq p_1 L_{1i}^2 C_{1i}$. With SIC, receiver i will decode the signals in the order of $q, q-1, \cdots, n$. The intended signal n is decodable, if both the intended and stronger unintended signals satisfy the SINR threshold.

Define the so-called residual SINR (rSINR) [9] as the mathematical program as follow: $rSINR_{ji}[t] = \dfrac{p_j \cdot L_{ji}^2 \cdot C_{ji}}{\sum_{Q=1}^{Q-1} p_q \cdot L_{qi}^2 \cdot D_{jqi} + N_0}$, where the summation in the denominator includes all transmit nodes q with weaker received signals than node j, $C_{ji} = min_q \left\| (v_{ji}^q)' H_{ji}' u_j^q \right\|^2$, $D_{jki} = max_q \left\| (v_{ji}^q)' H_{ki}' U_k \right\|^2$. For intended node n, $C_{ni} = 1$ due to the SM requirements.

3.3   SIC-IA Based MIMO DoF Model

In general, a receiver may receive a aggregate signal from both the intended and unintended transmitters, receiver i divides the signals from they into five sets. **Set 1.** Unintended signals are canceled by DoFs at the transmitters. **Set 2.** Unintended signals are canceled by DoFs or IA at the receiver. **Set 3.** Unintended signals are decoded and subtracted from the composite received signals by SIC (i.e., the received powers from these transmitters are greater than the powers from the intended transmitter n). **Set 4.** Intended signals from intended node n. **Set 5.** Unintended signals are treated as noise for SIC (i.e., the received powers from these transmitters are less than the powers from intended node n).

For the unintended signals, the question of which sets (1, 2, 3 and 5) the signals belong to will be solved by an optimization problem. Now we describes the process of SIC scheme. First, $set1$ signals are canceled by IC and a part of $set2$ are canceled by IA. Then, the remaining composite signals are received at node i. A receiver has one reconfigurable receive matrix, which is updated iteratively during SIC. In each SIC iteration, the receiver first tries to use SIC to decode the signal. If the decoding is unsuccessful, it then tries to use IC to eliminate the interference; and if there are enough freedom resources, the signal will be eliminated and continues SIC decoding, otherwise the subsequent signals can not be decoded and will be decoded in the next time slice.

Now, we show how the joint IA and SIC model and DoF IC model can be coupled together. For the 5 sets of signals, we define three binary indicator variables $\gamma_{ji}[t]$ (for sets 1 and 2), $\eta_{ij}[t]$ (for sets 3 and 5) and $\lambda_{ji}[t]$ (for set 4).

$\gamma_{ji}[t] = 1$ if the interference from transmitter j to receiver i is canceled by DoF (either at node j or i), and 0 otherwise. When $\gamma_{ji}[t] = 1$, it does not determine which node does the IC (node j or i). Thus, we need the value of $\theta_{ji}[t]$ [9]. This sufficient condition can be modeled as follow: $x_j[t], y_i[t] \geq \gamma_{ji}[t]$.

$\eta_{ji}[t] = 1$ if the interference from unintended transmitter j to receiver i is canceled by SIC, and 0 otherwise. Similarly, we have: $x_j[t], y_i[t] \geq \eta_{ji}[t]$.

$\lambda_{ji}[t] = 1$ if intended transmitter j transmits data streams to node i via SM, and 0 otherwise. For SM, we have: $\lambda_{ji}[t] \leq z_l[t] \leq N_A \cdot \lambda_{ji}[t]$.

Now, we introduce the details about the MIMO DoF model with joint IA and SIC. With the above definitions for $\gamma_{ji}[t]$, $\eta_{ji}[t]$ and $\lambda_{ji}[t]$, the DoF consumption constraints in (2) and (3) can be extended by taking into account SIC. When node i is a transmit node, then the DoF consumption at this node must satisfy:

$$\sum_{l \in L_i^{out}} z_{(l)}[t] + \sum_{j \in \mathcal{I}_i} \theta_{ji}[t]\gamma_{ij}[t] \sum_{k \in \mathcal{I}_j^{in}}^{Tx(k) \neq i} z_{(k)}[t] \tag{5}$$
$$\leq N_A \cdot x_i[t] + (1 - x_i[t])B_i, (i \in \mathcal{N}, 1 \leq t \leq T),$$

where B_i is no small than the number of inference signal, we set $B_i = N_A \cdot |\mathcal{I}_i|$. Similarly, the DoF consumption at node i must satisfy:

$$\sum_{l \in L_i^{in}} z_{(k)}[t] + \sum_{j \in I_i} \theta_{ji}[t]\gamma_{ji}[t] \sum_{l \in L_j^{out}}^{Rx(l) \neq i} [\alpha_{kj}[t] - \beta_{kj}[t]] \tag{6}$$
$$\leq N_A \cdot y_i[t] + (1 - y_i[t])B_i, (i \in \mathcal{N}, 1 \leq t \leq T).$$

With DoF IC, the barrier signals can be removed and SIC can continue to work. We incorporate DoF IC into the rSINR definition through the $\eta_{ji}[t]$ and $\lambda_{ji}[t]$ variables, which allows us to account for only those interference signals handled by SIC. Thus, $rSINR_{ji}[t]$ can be re-defined as: $rSINR_{ji}[t] = \dfrac{p_j \cdot L_{ji}^2 \cdot C_{ji}}{\sum_{k \in I_i, k \neq j, \eta_{ki}[t]=1 or \lambda_{ki}[t]=1}^{p_k L_{ki}^2 \cdot C_{ki} \leq p_j L_{ji}^2 \cdot C_{ji}} p_k L_{ki}^2 D_{jki} + N_0}$, if node j is the intended node, $C_{ji} = 1$.

Note that if $\lambda_{ni}[t] = 1$ (i.e., intended signals send from transmitter n to receiver i), we must have: (i) The $rSINR_{ji}[t]$ of all stronger received signals from unintended transmitters j with $\eta_{ji}[t] = 1$ are no less than the SINR threshold β; (ii) $rSINR_{ni}[t]$ is no less than β. If $\lambda_{ni}[t] = 1$, we have:

$$SINR_{ji}[t] \geq \beta, \quad (i \in \mathcal{N}, j \in \mathcal{I}_i, \eta_{ji}[t] = 1 \ or \ \lambda_{ji} = 1, 1 \leq t \leq T). \tag{7}$$

4   Performance Evaluation

4.1   A Throughput Maximization Problem

Suppose there is a set of active sessions $\mathcal{F}$. Denote $r(f)$ as the rate of session f and r_{min} as the minimum session rate among all sessions $\mathcal{F}$, i.e., $r_{min} \leq r(f)$ $(f \in \mathcal{F})$. Our objective is to maximize r_{min}.

Denote $r_l(f)$ as the amount of data rate on link l for session f. Denote $s(f)$ as the source nodes of session f, we have the flow routing constraint as follow:

$$\sum_{l \in L_i^{out}} r_l(f) = r(f). \tag{8}$$

At the intermediate relay node, we have the flow routing constraint as follow:

$$\sum_{l \in L_i^{in}} r_l(f) = \sum_{l \in L_i^{out}} r_l(f). \tag{9}$$

It can be verified that if (8) and (9) are satisfied, the constraint of destination node is also satisfied. So it is sufficient to have (8) and (9).

Since the aggregate data rate on link l cannot exceed the links average rate, we have the link capacity constraints as follow:

$$\sum_{f=1}^{F} r_l(f) \leq \frac{1}{T} \sum_{t=1}^{T} z_{(l)}[t]. \tag{10}$$

Putting all the constraints together, we have the following formulation for the throughput maximization problem.

OPT max r_{min}
s.t. $r_{min} \leq r(f)$, $(f \in F)$;
Half duplex constraint: (1);
Node activity constraints: (2), (3);
DoF consumption with joint IA and SIC: (5), (6);
Sequential SIC with IC: (7);
Flow balance and link capacity constraints: (8), (9), (10);
Variables: $x_i[t], y_i[t], z_{(l)}[t], \pi_i[t], \theta_{ji}[t], \eta_{ji}[t], \gamma_{ji}[t],$
$\lambda_{ji}[t], r_l(f), r(f)$;
Constants :$M, N, T, B_i, p_j, L_{ji}^2, \beta, N_0, C_{ji}, D_{jki}$

Through reformulation on (4), (5), (6) and (7), OPT can be reformulated into a mixed integer linear program (MILP) [10]. There exist highly efficient heuristics to solve it. Another approach is to apply an off-the-shelf solver, like GUROBI, which can handle up to a moderate-sized network successfully. It is sufficient to demonstrate our results with moderate-sized networks, because the main goal of this paper is to explore joint IA and SIC for MIMO DoF.

4.2   A 50-Node Example

In this chapter, we will exploit this model to achieve two goals: (i) show how IA and SIC are performed in a network; (ii) make a quantitative comparison between our joint IA and SIC framework and the case without SIC.

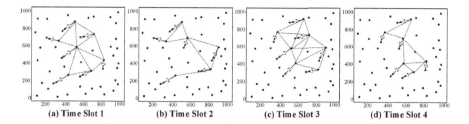

Fig. 2. Scheduled links in each time slots.

For generality, we normalize all units for location, data rate and power with appropriate dimensions. We consider a randomly generated wireless network with 50 nodes distributed in a 1000×1000 area. At the network layer, minimum-hop routing is employed, and there are 4 active sessions: N_7 to N_2, N_{19} to N_{50}, N_{10} to N_{43}, and N_{47} to N_{49}. We assume $M = 4$, $\beta = 1$ and $T = 4$. The transmit power is set to 1. The path-loss factor L_{ji}^2 between nodes i and j is $L_{ji}^2 = d_{ji}^{-\lambda}$, where d_{ji} is the Euclidean distance between the two nodes and $\lambda = 3$ is the path-loss index. The power of ambient noise is $N_0 = 10^{-10}$. The average value of C_{ji} is 0.3460. The worst case upper bound value for D_{jki} is 7.3753. For the 50-node network, we apply GORUBI solver for the MILP formulation.

Figure 2 demonstrates the transmission/reception pattern and interference pattern in each time slot. Specifically, a solid line with arrow represents a transmission link. A dashed line represents an interference. We get $r_{min} = 2$, which is a significantly improvement compared with the case without SIC ($r_{min} = 1$). Meanwhile, we get $E_j = 63$ and $E_{IA} = 43$, where denote E_j and E_{IA} as the number of eliminated interference signals in joint scheme and the number of eliminated interference signals in IA-MIMO scheme, respectively.

4.3   Complete Results

Table 1 shows r_{min} and E under the scheme for 60 randomly generated network instances. The total average percentage increase in r_{min} under the joint scheme is 100%, while the total average percentage of eliminated interference signals increase is 44.5%. Note that if all nodes with $r_l(f) = 1$ increase their $r_l(f)$ to 2, r_{min} will increase from 1 to 2. These increases are intuitive as less interference signals will remain more DoFs to transmit data and time slots for scheduling, so alleviating the DoF resources shortage issue.

Table 1. Optimized Results

Instances	1–20		21–40		41–60	
	r_{min}	E	r_{min}	E	r_{min}	E
IA-SIC in MIMO	2	E_j:59.0	2	E_j:62.4	2	E_j:61.5
Only IA in MIMO	1	E_{IA}:39.8	2	E_{IA}:44.3	1	E_{IA}:42.5

5   Conclusions

In multi-hop MIMO networks, since interference is unavoidable, DoF is a precious resource for SM and IC. This paper proposes a strategy joint IA and SIC to maximize the throughput in the multi-hop MIMO networks. For a transmitter, we will precode signals for IA and SIC to allow that the intended node receive more data streams. For a receiver, a part of inference signals will be aligned at the antennas and multiple signals are received by SIC. We studied the mathematical model to characterize (i) how the SINR threshold can be satisfied by using IA and IC; (ii) how DoF resources can be conserved by using IA and SIC. Based on our mathematical model, we studied a throughput maximization problem and confirmed that IA, SIC and IC can achieve the benefits proposed in this paper.

References

1. Biglieri, E., Calderbank, R., Constantinides, A., Goldsmith, A., Paulraj, A., Poor, H.V.: MIMO Wireless Communications. Cambridge University Press, New York (2007)
2. Shi, Y., Liu, J., Jiang, C., Gao, C., Hou, Y.T.: A DoF-based link layer model for multi-hop MIMO networks. IEEE Trans. Mob. Comput. **13**(99), 1395–1408 (2014)
3. Zeng, H., et al.: OFDM-based interference alignment in single-antenna cellular wireless networks. Proc. IEEE Trans. Commun. **65**(10), 4492–4506 (2017)
4. Li, L.E., Alimi, R., Shen, D., Viswanathan, H., Yang, Y.R.: A general algorithm for interference alignment and cancellation in wireless networks. In: Proceedings of the ACM WUWNet, Rome, Italy (2014)
5. Verdu, S.: Multiuser Detection. Cambridge University Press, Cambridge (1998)
6. Jiang, C., et al.: Cross-layer optimization for multi-hop wireless networks with successive interference cancellation. IEEE Trans. Wirel. Commun. **17**, 5819–5831 (2018)
7. Jalaeian, B., Shi, Y., Yuan, X., Hou, Y.T., Lou, W., Midkiff, S.F.: Harmonizing SIC and MIMO DoF interference cancellation for efficient network-wide resource allocation. In: Proceedings of the IEEE MASS, Dallas, Texas, pp. 316–323 (2015)
8. Lv, S., Zhuang, W., Xu, M., Wang, X., Liu, C., Zhou, X.: Understanding the scheduling performance in wireless networks with successive interference cancellation. IEEE Trans. Mob. Comput. **12**(8), 16251639 (2013)
9. Jalaian, B.A., et al.: On the integration of SIC and MIMO DoF for interference cancellation in wireless networks. Wireless Netw. **24**(7), 2357–2374 (2017). https://doi.org/10.1007/s11276-017-1472-7
10. Sherali, H.D., Adams, W.P.: A Reformulation Linearization Technique for Solving Discrete and Continuous Nonconvex Problems. Kluwer Academic Publishers, Dordrecht (1999)

A Novel Solution to Quality of Service Dilemma in Crowdsourcing Systems

Rui Zhang, Hui Xia$^{(\boxtimes)}$, Jufu Cui, and Xiangguo Cheng$^{(\boxtimes)}$

College of Computer Science and Technology, Qingdao University,
Qingdao 266100, China
xiahui@qdu.edu.cn

Abstract. Crowdsourcing recruits workers to finish complicated tasks, but it is prone to the quality of service dilemma, that is, the platform cannot guarantee the workers' quality of service. To solve this problem, we develop a novel quality of service improvement scheme. Firstly, to promote the workers cooperation, we propose an auction screening algorithm to estimate the rational quotation range of workers for screening workers and design a task reward function to motivate the workers to complete tasks. Secondly, to promote the platforms cooperation, we divide the rewards to the workers from the platforms into three categories and punish the platform that plays the defective strategy. Finally, the detailed experimental results show that the new scheme increases worker's reward to complete tasks and relieves the quality of service dilemma in the crowdsourcing system effectively.

Keywords: Quality of service · Cooperation · Auction screening

1 Introduction

Crowdsourcing [1–4] uses collective intelligence to finish complicated tasks that cannot be done simply by machines without participation of human intelligence. However, when the crowdsourcing platform recruiting workers to complete tasks, it is confronted with quality of service dilemma which restricts the efficient application of crowdsourcing system [5]. Therefore, we need to enhance workers' quality of service for solving the quality of service dilemma.

The methods to improve worker's quality of service can be divided into two categories: screening high level workers and designing attractive tasks. The former emphasizes on worker's reputation and ability and requires to check on worker's ability to see if he can complete the task successfully [6–9]. However, current worker screening schemes mainly focused on specific application area and

H. Xia—Supported by the National Natural Science Foundation of China (NSFC) under Grant No. 61872205, the Shandong Provincial Natural Science Foundation under Grant No. ZR2019MF018, and the Source Innovation Program of Qingdao under Grant No. 18-2-2-56-jch.

D. Yu et al. (Eds.): WASA 2020, LNCS 12385, pp. 105–112, 2020.
https://doi.org/10.1007/978-3-030-59019-2_12

most of them work well on certain kind of tasks and work poorly on other tasks. The latter have three main aspects: designing user interface, decomposing of task, and adopting incentive method [10–14]. However, the current task design method relies heavily on basic quality control techniques, the crowdsourcing platform cannot independently design the tasks based on its different needs.

Inspired by above schemes, this paper proposes a new quality of service improvement scheme to promote cooperation between workers and platforms for solving the quality of service dilemma. The main contributions are as follows:

(1) To promote the workers to play cooperative strategy, this paper designs an auction screening algorithm. This algorithm analogizes the definition of correlation coefficient to define grey distance and calculates worker's rational quotation range to pick high level workers in the range;
(2) To promote the platforms to play cooperative strategy, this paper divides the rewards paid to the workers from the platform into three categories: service quality reward, completion time reward, and extra reward, and punishes the platform that adopts defective strategy to encourage platforms to actively cooperate with workers;
(3) The detailed experiment results show that the new scheme improves worker's reward when completing the task and worker's service quality, and lowers the platform's cost when employing workers to complete the task.

2   Quality of Service Improvement Scheme

This section introduces how to promote cooperation between the platform and the workers.

2.1   Promote the Workers Play Cooperative Strategy

After the platform decides to complete the task with the assistance of workers, it will hang out the task and announce the task reward, the worker selects the task that they are interested in and submits their quotation to the platform. Usually, there will be many workers competing for the same task, so the platform needs to screen out high-quality workers to complete the task. In order to evaluate workers' quotation, this paper proposes an auction screening algorithm based on grey interval estimation model to estimate workers' rational quotation interval. In this algorithm, we analog the definition of correlation coefficient $c_x(r_{max}, r'_x(y))$ to define grey distance $dc_x(r, r'_x(y))$ that is,

$$
c_x(r_{max}, r'_x(y)) = \frac{\min\limits_{x=2}^{n-1}\{\min\limits_{y=2}^{m-1}\{|r'_x(m-1) - r'_x(y)|\}\} + \rho \max\limits_{x=2}^{n-1}\{\max\limits_{y=2}^{m-1}\{|r_{max} - r'_x(y)|\}\}}{|r'_x(m-1) - r'_y(y)| + \rho \max\limits_{x=2}^{n-1}\{\max\limits_{y=2}^{m-1}\{|r_{max} - r'_x(y)|\}\}}
$$

$$(1)$$

$$dc_x(r, r_x'(y)) = \frac{\min\limits_{x=2}^{n-1}\{\min\limits_{y=2}^{m-1}\{|r - r_x'(y)|\}\} + \rho\max\limits_{x=2}^{n-1}\{\max\limits_{y=2}^{m-1}\{|r - r_x'(y)|\}\}}{|r - r_x'(y)| + \rho\max\limits_{x=2}^{n-1}\{\max\limits_{y=2}^{m-1}\{|r - r_x'(y)|\}\}} \quad (2)$$

Where, $x = 2, \cdots, n - 1$, $y = 2, \cdots, m - 1$, r_{max} is the maximum value of each column in matrix, ρ is distinguishing coefficient, r is an estimate of the workers' quotation. And then we use the grey confidence level α to calculate workers' rational price range $[r_0, r_1]$ based on worker's historical quotation of same tasks, the detailed process is shown in Algorithm 1.

Algorithm 1: Auction Screening Algorithm

Input: the workers' historical quotations set R, the distinguishing coefficient ρ, and the confidence coefficient α

Output: The quotations range of the workers $[r_0, r_1]$

01: Transform the historical quotations sample set R to the matrix R'

02: Take the maximum value of each column in R' as the reference sequence $r_{max} = \{r_x'(m - 1), u = 2, \ldots, n - 1\}$ and standardize the matrix R'

03: Calculate the correlation coefficient $c_x(r_{max}, r_x'(y))$

04: Normalize $c_x(r_{max}, r_c'(y))$ to obtain correlation degree w_x

05: Take the value of mean in each column element of R' and calculate the gray estimate r of the workers' quotation with $r = \sum\limits_{x=2}^{n-1} w_x * \bar{r}_x$

06: Calculate the quotations range of the workers $[r_0, r_1]$ with

07:      $dc_x(r, r_x'(y)) \geq \alpha$

The process of transforming the historical quotations sample set R to the matrix $R'_{m\times n}$ can be described as: the data of historical quotations set R are written the matrix $R'_{m\times n}$ in columns, sorted the matrix $R'_{m\times n}$ in ascending order, and deleted the edge data of $R'_{m\times n}$ to obtain the matrix $R'_{(m-1)\times(n-1)}$. That is,

$$R'_{(m-1)\times(n-1)} = (r_2'(y), ..., r_{n-1}'(y)) = \begin{bmatrix} r_2'(2) & r_3'(2) & \cdots & r_{n-1}'(2) \\ r_2'(3) & r_3'(3) & \cdots & r_{n-1}'(3) \\ \vdots & \vdots & \vdots & \vdots \\ r_2'(m-1) & r_3'(m-1) & \cdots & r_{n-1}'(m-1) \end{bmatrix} \quad (3)$$

However, although we use an auction screening algorithm to screen the workers with high-quality for completing the tasks, it cannot guarantee that the selected high-quality workers will complete the task on time and with good quality. Therefore, we design a quality service reward function $q_w^i(q_i)$ and a completion time reward function $t_w^i(t_i)$,

$$q_w^i(q_i) = sign(q_i - q_0) * \frac{q_i}{\sum\limits_{z=1}^{n} q_z} * r^q \tag{4}$$

$$t_w^i(t_i) = sign(t_i - t_0) * \frac{e^{-t_i}}{\sum\limits_{z=1}^{n} e^{-t_z}} * r^t \tag{5}$$

Where $sign(x)$ refers to the symbolic function and satisfy

$$sign(q_i - q_0) = \begin{cases} 1, q_i - q_0 \geq 0 \\ -1, q_i - q_0 < 0 \end{cases} , sign(t_i - t_0) = \begin{cases} 1, t_0 - t_i \geq 0 \\ -1, t_0 - t_i < 0 \end{cases}$$

Where q_0 and t_0 are the service quality level threshold value and the completion time threshold value respectively, r^q and r^t are the service quality reward and the completion time reward respectively.

2.2   Promote the Platforms to Play Cooperative Strategy

When the platform employs workers to complete the task, the workers hope to get more rewards from the platform at the lowest cost, while the platform wants to get the most done with the least money. Thus, the interactions between the workers and the platforms can be modeled as a two-person game model. For the rational workers and platforms, they will actively seek a strategy to maximize their payoff. However, the two players are too selfish to actively play cooperation strategy (i.e., the worker completes tasks with high quality and timely for the platform and the platform pays rewards to workers for completing tasks), so we need to take some incentive measures to promote the cooperation between workers and platforms.

To solve this problem, this paper divides the rewards to the workers from the platforms into three types of rewards, i.e., worker's quality service reward q_w, worker's completion time reward t_w, and platform's extra reward e_p, and then punishes strictly the platform that plays the defective strategy. The platform's extra reward refers to the difference between the worker's estimated cost of completing tasks and worker's actual cost of completing tasks. We use the reward function $q_w^i(q_i)$ and $t_w^i(t_i)$ to calculate the worker's quality service reward q_w and completion time reward t_w. The payoff matrix of two players can be modified to Table 1.

Where W is the worker, P is the platform. C_W means that the worker completes tasks on time and with good quality for the platform; D_W means that the worker completes tasks with low quality or delays for the platform. C_P means that the platform pays rewards to workers for completing tasks; D_P means that the platform does not pay rewards to workers for completing tasks. q_i is the service quality level when the worker i completes the task, t_i is the time taken by the worker i to complete the task, $q_w^c(q_i)$ and $q_w^d(q_i{}')$ are the service quality reward obtained by workers playing C and playing D respectively, $t_w^c(t_i)$ and $t_w^d(t_i{}')$ are the completion time reward obtained by playing C and playing D respectively. From Table 1, if

Table 1. Payoff matrix

Payoff $W\backslash P$	C_P	D_P
C_W	$q_w^c(q_i) + t_w^c(t_i) - c_w - e_p,\ u - q_w^c(q_i) - t_w^c(t_i) + e_p$	$-c_w,\ u - e_p$
D_W	$q_w^d(q_i{}') + t_w^d(t_i{}'),\ -q_w^d(q_i{}') - t_w^d(t_i{}')$	$0, 0$

$$\begin{cases} q_w^c(q_i) + t_w^c(t_i) - c_w - e_p > q_w^d(q_i{}') + t_w^d(t_i{}') \\ u - q_w^c(q_i) - t_w^c(q_i) + e_p > u - e_p \end{cases} \tag{6}$$

The *Nash equilibrium* of this game is the strategy profile (*worker C, platform C*). Assume $c_w < q_w^c(q_i) + t_w^c(t_i) - q_w^d(q_i') - t_w^d(t_i')$, we have,

$$\frac{q_w^i(q_i) + t_w^i(t_i)}{2} < e_p < q_w^i(q_i) + t_w^i(t_i) - q_w^i(q_i') - t_w^i(t_i') - c_w \tag{7}$$

The optimal strategies of the platform is cooperative strategies. Therefore, to promote the platform to play cooperative strategy, we can set the proper service quality threshold and completion time threshold to make the payoff of two players in the range of $\frac{q_w^i(q_i) + t_w^i(t_i)}{2} < e_p < q_w^i(q_i) + t_w^i(t_i) - q_w^i(q_i') - t_w^i(q_i') - c_w$.

3 Stimulation Results

This paper uses anaconda integrated development tool to verify the effectiveness of *q*uality of *s*ervice *i*mprovement *s*cheme *QSIS*. First, we analyze the variation trend of worker's reward after completing the task and platform's extra reward of different service quality threshold and completion time threshold; Second, we compare the worker's reward when he adopts *QSIS* and three classic interactive strategy: Winner (using winner's strategy), Loser (using loser's strategy) and Opponent (using opponent's strategy). The parameters of experiment is shown in Table 2.

Table 2. Parameter setting

Parameter	e	c_w	u	r^q	r^t	q		t	
Value	1	0.3	1.5	180	20	0.3	0.5	0.7	7	9

The comparison of workers' rewards: Fig. 1 displays the variation trend of worker's rewards when the threshold value (Quality of Service threshold and completion time threshold) are $t = 7, q = 0.3, 0.5, 0.7$ and $t = 9, q = 0.3, 0.5, 0.7$. Comparing Fig. 1(a) and Fig. 1(b), we can see that when t is fixed, the worker's reward when finishing the task decrease as q increases. This variation trend is related with the service quality reward function and the completion time reward function designed in this paper. In addition, in the process of simulating workers' interaction, we find out that if the reward of task completion time set by the platform occupies a large proportion in the general reward, the workers will gain more reward but this also means that the platform will spend too much cost when using the worker's labor, which might even exceed the general cost it expected at the very beginning. This cannot promote workers to actively cooperate. Therefore, we set r^q and r^t to be 180 and 20.

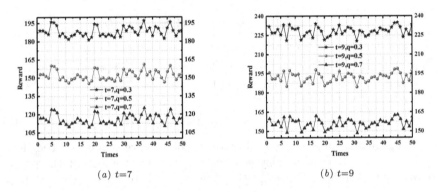

(a) t=7   (b) t=9

Fig. 1. Reward for workers who complete the task.

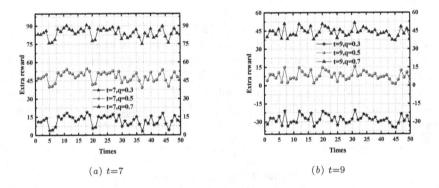

(a) t=7   (b) t=9

Fig. 2. Extra reward that platform gains.

The comparison of platform's extra reward: Fig. 2 displays the variation trend of the extra reward that platform gains when using the labor of workers when the threshold value are $t = 7, q = 0.3, 0.5, 0.7$ and $t = 9, q = 0.3, 0.5, 0.7$. By comparing Fig. 2(a) and Fig. 2(b), we can see that when t is fixed, the extra reward that platform will gain by using labors of workers increases as q increases, and when q is fixed, the extra reward that platform will gain by using labors of workers decreases as t increases. This variation trend is also related to the two reward function designed in this paper.

The comparison of worker's reward: Table 3 compares the income when worker adopts $QSIS$ ($t = 7, q = 0.5$) and three classic interactive strategy. According to the total income of 10 times of interaction by four different strategies, we can see that $QSIS$ makes the highest payoff, followed by Opponent and the Loser makes the lowest payoff. This is because $QSIS$ pays the worker reward according to his service quality and task completion time. Only when those two factors both meet the requirement of platform, the worker will be rewarded by the platform. Therefore, $QSIS$ can encourage workers to finish the task in time and with good quality.

Table 3. Comparison of worker's reward

Number	$QSIS$	Winner	Loser	Opponent
1	0.21	−0.3	−0.3	−0.3
2	0.21	0	−0.3	1
3	0.09	0	−0.3	−0.3
4	0.41	0	−0.3	1
5	0.04	0	−0.3	−0.3
6	0.18	0	−0.3	1
7	0.9	0	−0.3	−0.3
8	0.97	0	−0.3	1
9	0.41	0	−0.3	−0.3
10	0.97	0	−0.3	1
Total payoff	4.39	−0.3	−3	3.5

4 Conclusion

Solving the service quality dilemma for improving the worker's quality of service is the key to promote the efficient application of crowdsourcing system. This paper proposes a quality of service improvement scheme to solve this problem. To begin with, this paper proposes an auction screening algorithm to screen workers with high-quality and designs a task reward function to motivate the workers to complete the task on time and with high quality. Next, this paper divides the rewards that paid to the workers into three categories and punishes the platform that plays defective strategy to promote the platforms cooperation. Finally, detailed simulation experiments verify the effectiveness of new scheme.

In the future research, we will design new quality of service improvement schemes to solve the problem of the service quality dilemma.

References

1. Kittur, A., Smus, B., Khamkar, S., Kraut, R.E.: Crowdforge: crowdsourcing complex work. In: Proceedings of the 24th Annual ACM Symposium on User Interface Software and Technology, pp. 43–52 (2011)
2. Cai, Z., Duan, Z., Li, W.: Exploiting multi-dimensional task diversity in distributed auctions for mobile crowdsensing. IEEE Trans. Mob. Comput. (2020). https://doi. org/10.1109/TMC.2020.2987881
3. Duan, Z., Li, W., Zheng, X., Cai, Z.: Mutual-preference driven truthful auction mechanism in mobile crowdsensing. In: Proceedings of the 39th IEEE International Conference on Distributed Computing Systems (ICDCS), pp. 1233–1242 (2019)
4. Duan, Z., Li, W., Cai, Z.: Distributed auctions for task assignment and scheduling in mobile crowdsensing systems. In: Proceedings of the 37th IEEE International Conference on Distributed Computing Systems (ICDCS), pp. 635–644 (2017)
5. Acosta, M., Zaveri, A., Simperl, E., Kontokostas, D., Flick, F., Lehmann, J.: Detecting linked data quality issues via crowdsourcing: a DBpedia study. J. Semant. Web 9(3), 303–335 (2018)
6. Whiting, M. E., Gamage, D., Gaikwad, S. S., Gilbee, A., Goyal, S., Ballav, A.: Crowd guilds: worker-led reputation and feedback on crowdsourcing platforms. In: Proceedings of the 2017 ACM Conference on Computer Supported Cooperative Work and Social Computing, pp. 1902–1913 (2017)
7. Gaikwad, S.S., Morina, D., Ginzberg, A., Mullings, C., Goyal, S., Gamage, D.: Boomerang: rebounding the consequences of reputation feedback on crowdsourcing platforms. In: Proceedings of the 29th Annual Symposium on User Interface Software and Technology, pp. 625–637 (2016)
8. Das Sarma, A., Parameswaran, A., Widom, J.: Towards globally optimal crowdsourcing quality management: the uniform worker setting. In: Proceedings of the 2016 International Conference on Management of Data, pp. 47–62 (2016)
9. Kazai, G., Zitouni, I.: Quality management in crowdsourcing using gold judges behavior. In: Proceedings of the Ninth ACM International Conference on Web Search and Data Mining, pp. 267–276 (2016)
10. Campo, S., Khan, V.J., Papangelis, K., Markopoulos, P.: Community heuristics for user interface evaluation of crowdsourcing platforms. Future Gen. Comput. Syst. 95, 775–789 (2019)
11. Tong, Y., Chen, L., Zhou, Z., Jagadish, H.V., Shou, L., Lv, W.: SLADE: a smart large-scale task decomposer in crowdsourcing. IEEE Trans. Knowl. Data Eng. 30(8), 1588–1601 (2018)
12. Ni, J., Zhang, K., Yu, Y., Lin, X., Shen, X.: Providing task allocation and secure deduplication for mobile crowdsensing via fog computing. IEEE Trans. Dependable Secure Comput. 17(3) (2018)
13. Wang, Y., Jia, X., Jin, Q., Ma, J.: QuaCentive: a quality-aware incentive mechanism in mobile crowdsourced sensing (MCS). J. Supercomput. 72(8), 2924–2941 (2015). https://doi.org/10.1007/s11227-015-1395-y
14. Li, J., Cai, Z., Yan, M., Li, Y.: Using crowdsourced data in location-based social networks to explore influence maximization. In: Proceedings of the 35th Annual IEEE International Conference on Computer Communications, pp. 1–9 (2016)

C-DAG: Community-Assisted DAG Mechanism with High Throughput and Eventual Consistency

Zhujun Zhang[1,2]($\boxtimes$), Dali Zhu[1], and Baoxin Mi[1]

[1] Institute of Information Engineering, Chinese Academy of Sciences, Beijing, China
zhangzhujun@iie.ac.cn
[2] School of Cyber Security, University of Chinese Academy of Sciences, Beijing, China

Abstract. Blockchain provides a trust model applied to distributed networks, which can achieve strong consistency under decentralized conditions according to its serial chain structure and consensus algorithm. However, the scalability bottleneck limits practical applications. Directed Acyclic Graph (DAG) technology can greatly improve the scalability of system, but it also inevitably incurs security and consistency issues. For addressing the above issues, this paper proposes Community-assisted DAG (C-DAG) model, which can achieve the following advantages: (1) High throughput. Based on Clauset-Newman-Moore (CNM) community detection algorithm, the closely connected network entity nodes are divided into a community. Through the DAG-based parallel transactions in the community, the throughput is greatly improved. (2) Eventual consistency. POV-combined PBFT consensus adopted inside the community and the event-driven global block sequencing algorithm applied between the communities guarantee the convergence and final consistency of C-DAG. The paper finally verifies the high throughput and low latency of C-DAG consensus based on simulation experiments.

Keywords: C-DAG · CNM · Consensus mechanism · Throughput · Consistency

1 Introduction

Blockchain technology has a highly decentralized nature [1]. The basic unit of a chained blockchain is a block. Blocks are connected by hash pointers, which ensure data integrity, continuity, and legality. However, the cost of blockchain decentralized trust mechanism is the scalability bottleneck. The performance bottleneck of the blockchain is mainly caused by its consensus mechanism [2]. The essential idea is that the nodes of the entire network compete for the right to keep accounts. The nodes that successfully obtain the accounting rights confirm the transaction. The consensus greatly limits the blockchain throughput [3].

Compared with the chain-type blockchain, the directed acyclic graph (DAG) [4] has superior scalability. The chained blockchain is limited by the chained organization of data, and any bifurcation will be considered illegal [5]. The uniqueness of the authority to write to the database and the unidirectional extension of the data greatly limits the

© Springer Nature Switzerland AG 2020
D. Yu et al. (Eds.): WASA 2020, LNCS 12385, pp. 113–121, 2020.
https://doi.org/10.1007/978-3-030-59019-2_13

scalability and concurrency of the blockchain. In terms of data organization, the DAG-style blockchain allows two or more hash pointers one block, and blocks within a period of time will form a directed acyclic graph. In terms of write permissions, the DAG-style blockchain allows multiple users to have write permissions. The producer of each block can choose to refer to multiple historical blocks independently, and then broadcast the transaction. The user who receives the block will save it in the local database. Reforming of these two aspects has made DAG blockchains greatly improved in scalability and concurrency.

As a rumor spreading algorithm [6], DAG asynchronous mechanism not only improves scalability but also brings uncontrollable problems of consistency. Blockchain is a verification mechanism for synchronous operation, which can ensure a high consistency [7]. However, as an asynchronous operation, DAG does not have a global sorting mechanism. When running a smart contract, it is likely that the data stored between nodes will deviate from the original ones after a period of operation.

In response to above problems, we design C-DAG model to achieve a balance between scalability and security. Specifically, contributions of this work are as follows:

- Constructing C-DAG architecture. C-DAG is a community-based distributed ledger technology, and it divides the distributed ledger into two categories: one is a local distributed ledger, which is maintained by communities composed of network nodes with close communication, improving system throughput through the DAG parallel mechanism; the other is the global distributed ledger, which only synchronizes global data when transactions are generated between communities.
- Proposing community division algorithm based on weighted CNM. A reasonable community division is a prerequisite for ensuring concurrent performance. We take the communication data as the weight of the edges between the nodes, and introduce the weight into the CNM algorithm. By running the weighted CNM, the nodes with close transactions are divided into the same community.
- Designing a community-based consensus mechanism. C-DAG takes the Practical Byzantine Fault Tolerance (PBFT) consensus algorithm combined with proof of vote (POV) [8] to ensure the consistency of local distributed ledger inside the community. At the same time, a global block ranking mechanism based on inter-community transaction events is introduced to guarantee the final consistency of global distributed ledger.

2 Related Work

To solve the scalability bottleneck of traditional blockchains, dozens of DAG-based distributed ledgers have been proposed. DAG-Chain saves time for packaging transactions and blocks, and theoretically obtains a qualitative leap in efficiency.

From the macroscopic view of graph theory topology model, DAG realizes an innovation from single chain to tree and mesh, from block granularity refinement to transaction granularity, and from single point transition to concurrent writing. DAG's current representative projects include IOTA [9], byteball [10], nano [11] and so on. IOTA is a distributed ledger for the Internet of Things (IoT). IOTA takes PoW to calculate weight and cumulative weight for each transaction [12]. Because there is no miner incentive [13], IOTA is vulnerable to denial of service attacks. Byteball is known as the representative of Blockchain 3.0. It innovatively introduces the concept of main chain and witnesses [14]. The disadvantage of Byteball is the uncertain time of transaction confirmation [15]. Nano is a new type of cryptocurrency based on block lattice [16]. Nano innovatively adopts a user-one-chain approach, only recording its own transactions, and does not share data with other accounts, so that all transactions can be executed in concurrency, providing second-level transaction speed. Nano adopts DPOS for consensus [17].

New DAG projects are also emerging, such as HashGraph [18], Conflux [19], DEXON [20], SPECTRE [21], PHANTOM [22], etc. Some of these technologies have improvements in consensus algorithms and concurrency, but there is also a general consistency problem in concurrency mechanisms. Therefore, it is necessary to take advantages of DAG's scalability and fully consider the consistency issues, which is also the focus of this paper.

3   C-DAG Architecture

C-DAG must achieve the following design goals concerning security and performance.

High Throughput: Eliminating the problems of poor scalability and low throughput of traditional blockchain networks. By introducing the DAG with concurrency mechanism, the throughput under decentralized conditions will be increased.

Consistency: It is necessary to clarify the consensus mechanism and the data synchronization method to ensure the consistency of the global network node account.

Based on the target requirements, we adopt the DAG-based concurrency mechanism to meet the system scalability. In the actual network, some network entity nodes interact closely, as well as there are few transactions between some other network entity nodes. It is not necessary to maintain strong consistency of all network data, while maintaining the final consistency can meet system requirements. Therefore, in order to optimize the resource consumption and improve the system throughput while using the advantages of DAG to achieve consensus and decentralization, this paper designs a C-DAG architecture based on the idea of community division, as shown in Fig. 1.

The principles of C-DAG include two aspects: (1) Introducing the concept of community. Based on community analysis algorithm, divide closely connected nodes into a unified community. The DAG concurrency mechanism is adopted inside the community to improve system throughput. (2) By running an independent consensus mechanism within the community and a global block ranking mechanism driven by transactions between communities, the global final consistency is guaranteed.

4   CNM-Assisted Community Building Algorithm

A reasonable community division method is a necessary prerequisite for improving network concurrency. A community is a collection of device nodes that are closely connected and have certain common characteristics in the network.

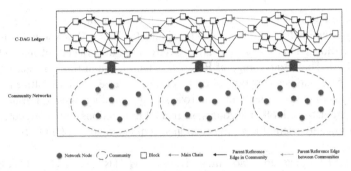

Fig. 1. C-DAG architecture.

Typical algorithms for community division include: Clauset-Newman-Moore algorithm (CNM) [23], Louvain [24], Label Propagation Algorithm (LPA) [25], etc. Although clustering algorithms such as Louvain have high flexibility and fast speed, it is inevitable to calculate the eigenvalues of the matrix, which requires a large amount of calculation. In addition, the results of LPA algorithms are unstable. Therefore, in this paper, the greedy algorithm CNM algorithm based on modularity Q optimization with high stability proposed by Newman is adopted to divide communities. The excellent degree of community division is measured by the modularity Q.

The original definition of modularity Q is as follows:

$$Q = \sum_i (e_{ii} - a_i^2) \tag{1}$$

As in the formula above, e_{ii} is the inner edge density of community i, a_i is the edge density of one end node in community i and the other is outside. Q represents the comparison between the edge density in the community and cross the communities. The closer Q is to 1, the better the result of the division.

In order to realize the community division more accurately, the daily interaction data of two nodes is taken as the weight of the edge between them. The greater the amount of data interacted between nodes, the greater the weight, and the closer the relationship between the two nodes. Therefore, weight information is added to the Q calculation formula to more accurately measure the relationship between nodes. The improved Q calculation formula is defined as follows:

$$Q = \sum_i (e_{ii}w_{ii} - (a_iw_i)^2) \tag{2}$$

The newly added parameter w_{ii} is the weight of the connection between different nodes in the community i; w_i represents the weight of the connection between the internal nodes and the external nodes of the community i.

The principle of weighted CNM algorithm is to construct an incremental matrix of modularity Q, and then obtain a community structure of maximum Q by updating it. The basic steps of the CNM algorithm can refer to bibliography [23].

We take the network topology shown in Fig. 2 as an example. It is calculated by CNM algorithm based on weighted Q optimization. The results are shown in Fig. 3.

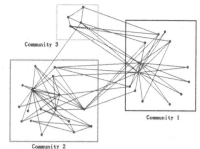

Fig. 2. Network example.   **Fig. 3.** Community division results.

In order to evaluate whether the divided communities are superior, the following factor need to be considered: whether Q is close to 1. The closer Q is to 1, the closer the nodes in the community are, and the more ideal the community is. Theoretically, the range of modularity Q is $[-1/2, 1)$, while the Q of the above example is 0.6179, which is closer to 1, the community division effect is rather reasonable.

5 C-DAG Consensus Mechanism

An important goal of this paper is to guarantee the security and consistency of C-DAG network through consensus mechanism. Based on the C-DAG architecture in Sect. 3.2, the C-DAG consensus mechanism is divided into two steps: (1) Designing the DAG-based POV-combined PBFT consensus algorithm (DVPBFT) that is suitable for weakly synchronous DAG environments in the community; (2) Adopting global data synchronization mechanism based on transactions between communities.

DVPBFT introduces a voting mechanism on the basis of PBFT, and implements the selection of nodes participating block production based on votes under weak synchronization environment.

In the DVPBFT algorithm, these nodes in one community are divided into three roles: voter, producer, and candidate (see Fig. 4).

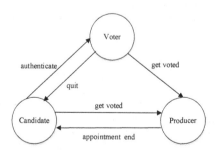

Fig. 4. DVPBFT model.

Voter: The voters are in charge of voting for producers. Voters are derived from candidates according to authentication.

Producer: The node that gets at least $1 + N_v/2$ notes (N_v is the number of voters) can become producer, and is responsible for producing blocks within a certain appointment period.

Candidate: Candidates can be authenticated as voters, or can become producers based on the voting results.

In the DVPBFT consensus preparation stage, each node applies for an ID to identify the identity. In the commit stage, a transaction block is randomly selected for voting, and all nodes participating in the consensus collect the voting results. In a weakly synchronized network environment, if a sufficient number of votes is not received after the end of a vote, the voter continues to vote until the voting result exceeds the voting threshold, recommends the blocks that can be produced, then the consensus in the community is completed.

A global data synchronization mechanism between communities is based on transaction. When there is a transaction between blocks, global data synchronization is triggered. The global data consensus algorithm can choose DVPBFT, nano or other asynchronous synchronization mechanism.

The community-based consensus mechanism proposed in this paper maintains independent consensus within the community, while global consensus only occurs when there is a transaction between communities. It is not necessary to maintain global data consistency in real time, which greatly improves the efficiency of consensus.

6   C-DAG Evaluation

Latency and throughput is a pair of indicators to measure scalability, so for evaluating the advantages of C-DAG in scalability, we mainly analyze the transaction throughput and consensus latency of DVPBFT. The specific code of each node is written in python, and the server node program is written based on the flask framework to simulate the consensus behavior of each node. The following experiment compares DVPBFT with PBFT (not combined with POV) and nano which is a representative of consensus protocol for the DAG ledger based on parallel chain.

For facilitating the comparative evaluation of consensus algorithm, we design the following scoring formula of scalability:

$$Scalability = \sum_{T} \frac{tps}{latency} \tag{3}$$

T is the number of consensus nodes; tps (transaction per second) is the transaction volume per second (equivalent to block generation volume per second), which can be expressed as $tps = \sum transactions / \triangle t$; $latency$ is the average consensus time.

Based on the above analysis, we select the communities with 10, 20, 30, 40, 50, 60, 70, 80, 90 and 100 nodes to experiment respectively, and observe the effectiveness of the consensus algorithm. The correlation results of DVPBFT are compared with the PBFT algorithm as shown in Fig. 5, Fig. 6, Fig. 7.

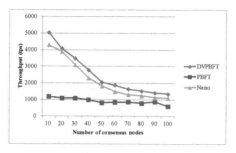

Fig. 5. Comparison of tps.

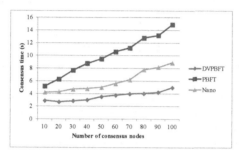

Fig. 6. Comparison of consensus time.

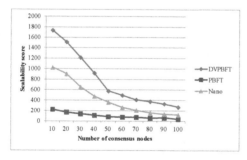

Fig. 7. Comparison of scalability score.

1) **Comparison of throughput.** As shown in Fig. 5, with the increase of deployed consensus nodes, the system throughput continues to decline due to server hardware conditions. Since DVPBFT is an asynchronous parallel consensus mechanism based on POV, which also does not need to wait for the miners to pack like the traditional blockchain, its throughput has been greatly improved with the average tps is 2521. The throughput of DVPBFT is much greater than PBFT (the average tps is 915). Meanwhile, because nano is based on POS, its transaction block size is larger than block size of DVPBFT which is POV assisted, DVPBFT throughput is also higher than nano (the average tps is 2164).

2) **Comparison of consensus time.** As shown in Fig. 6, with the number of node in a community increasing, the consensus time of DVPBFT maintains steady and slow growth, while the consensus time of PBFT is increasing sharply. DVPBFT consensus also takes less time-consuming than nano.

3) **Comparison of scalability value.** According to formula (3), we further compare the scalability improvement score of DVPBFT, PBFT and nano. Figure 7 shows the results. DVPBFT has better scalability than other two consensus algorithms.

7 Conclusion

In order to improve the throughput of blockchain network, this paper takes DTG technology to achieve network concurrency performance. Meanwhile, for solving the consistency problem brought by the parallel mechanism, this paper proposes C-DAG model, which can achieve a balance between scalability and security. C-DAG adopts community analysis algorithm CNM to construct community with closely communicated nodes, each community takes a distributed ledger technology based on DAG to improve system throughput. On the other hand, for addressing the issue of data consistency, independent consensus algorithm based on the DVPBFT is adopted within the community, and transaction-based data synchronization mechanism is adopted between the communities. The simulation analysis shows that the C-DAG implements obvious advantages in increasing throughput and shortening confirmation time, which has important reference value for distributed system.

Acknowledgment. This work was supported by the National Natural Science Foundation of China (Grant No.61502486).

References

1. Zhu, S., Cai, Z., Hu, H., Li, Y., Li, W.: zkCrowd: a hybrid blockchain-based crowdsourcing platform. IEEE Trans. Ind. Inform. (TII) **16**(6), 4196–4205 (2020)
2. Yan, Z.: Security architecture and key technologies of blockchain. J. Inf. Secur. Res. **2**(12), 1090–1097 (2016)
3. Kuzuno, H., Karam, C.: Blockchain explorer: an analytical process and investigation environment for bitcoin. In: Crime Researchers Summit, pp. 9–16 (2017)
4. Gao, Z.F., Zheng, J.L., Tang, S.Y., Long, Y.: State-of-the-art survey of consensus mechanisms on dag-based distributed ledger. J. Softw. **31**(4), 1124–1142 (2020)
5. Zhu, S., Li, W., Li, H., Tian, L., Luo, G., Cai, Z.: Coin hopping attack in blockchain-based IoT. IEEE Internet Things J. **6**(3), 4614–4626 (2019)
6. Shen, X., Pei, Q.: Overview of blockchain technology. J. Netw. Inf. Secur. **2**(11), 11–20 (2016)
7. Giacomo, B., Marco, P., Michele, A., Francesco, Z.: An adaptive peer-to-peer overlay scheme for location-based services. Netw. Comput. Appl. (NCA) **2**(1), 181–188 (2014)
8. Li, K.: Proof of vote a high-performance consensus protocol based on vote mechanism & consortium blockchain. In: IEEE International Conference on High Performance Computing (2017)
9. Chen, J., Siyu, C.: An intelligent task offloading algorithm (iTOA) for UAV edge computing network. Digit. Commun. Netw. (2020)

10. Churyumov, A.: Byteball: a decentralized system for storage and transfer of value (2016). https://byteball.org/Byteball.pdf
11. LeMahieu, C.: Nano: a feeless distributed cryptocurrency network (2018). https://nano.org/en/whitepaper
12. Kraft, Daniel: Difficulty control for blockchain-based consensus systems. Peer-to-Peer Netw. Appl. **9**(2), 397–413 (2015). https://doi.org/10.1007/s12083-015-0347-x
13. Yao, Y., Chang, X.: Decentralized identity authentication and key management scheme based on blockchain. Cyberspace Secur. **6**(10), 36–39 (2019)
14. Don, T., Alex, T.: How blockchain will change organizations. MIT Sloan Manag. Rev. **58**, 10–13 (2017)
15. Eyal, I., Gencer, A., Sirer, EG., Van, R.: Bitcoin-NG: a scalable blockchain protocol. In: Proceedings of the 13th USENIX Symposium on Networked Systems Design and Implementation (NSDI 2016), pp. 45–59 (2016)
16. King, S., Nadal, S.: Ppcoin: Peer-to-peer crypto-currency with proof-of-stake (2012). https://www.doc88.com/p-0788912122970.html
17. Benčić, FM., Žarko, IP.: Distributed ledger technology: blockchain compared to directed acyclic graph. In: Proceedings of the 38th IEEE International Conference on Distributed Computing Systems (ICDCS), pp. 1569–1570. IEEE (2018)
18. Baird, L.: The swirlds hashgraph consensus algorithm: Fair, fast, Byzantine fault tolerance. Technical Report, Swirlds Tech Reports SWIRLDS-TR-2016–01 (2016)
19. Li, C., Li, P., Xu, W., Long, F., Yao, A.: Scaling Nakamoto consensus to thousands of transactions per second. arXiv Preprint arXiv:1805.03870 (2018)
20. Chen, Y.: DEXON: a highly scalable, decentralized DAG-based consensus algorithm. arXiv Preprint arXiv:1811.07525 (2018)
21. Sompolinsky, Y., Lewenberg, Y., Zohar, A.: SPECTRE: serialization of proof-of-work events: Confirming transactions via recursive elections (2016). https://eprint.iacr.org/2016/1159.pdf
22. Sompolinsky, Y., Zohar, A.: PHANTOM: a scalable BlockDAG protocol. IACR Cryptology ePrint Archive (2018)
23. Clauset, A., Newman, M.E., Moore, C.: Finding community structure in very large networks. Phys. Rev. E **70**(6), 066111 (2004)
24. Blondel, V.D., et al.: Fast unfolding of communities in large networks. J. Stat. Mech.: Theory Exp. **2008**(10), P10008 (2008)
25. Raghavan, U.N., Albert, R., Kumara, S.: Near linear time algorithm to detect community structures in large-scale networks. Phys. Rev. E **76**(3), 036106 (2007)

Non-pre-trained Mine Pedestrian Detection Based on Automatic Generation of Anchor Box

Xing Wei, Changguang Wang$^{(\boxtimes)}$, Haitao Zhang, Shaofan Liu, and Yang Lu

Hefei University of Technology, Hefei, China
wcg1234wang@qq.com

Abstract. Mine pedestrian detection is an important part of computer vision and one of the key technologies of unmanned locomotive. In order to improve the structural adaptability of pedestrian detection network, reduce the workload of pre-training and reduce the risk of "negative migration" brought by migration learning, a non-pre-training underground pedestrian detection network based on anchor box is proposed. Firstly, the network model of mine pedestrian detection is introduced, including non-pretrained backbone network and branch structure detection network. Among them, the non-pre-trained backbone network mainly adds BatchNorm operation to make the gradient more stable and smooth. Anchor location prediction branch and anchor shape prediction branch in the detection network work together to improve the regression accuracy of anchor box. Secondly, the loss function of network training is described and the training parameters are adjusted by weighted loss. Finally, the experimental results based on the video of Taoyuan and Xinji mine in Anhui province are given. The experimental data show that the proposed algorithm can still maintain 96.3% AP at a real-time processing rate of 24 FPS. Compared with the RefineDet512, the AP increases by 2.4%.

Keywords: Mine pedestrian detection · Deep learning network · Anchor box detection

1 Introduction

Currently, the state-of-the-art object detection [1,2] uses the sliding window mechanism of the anchor box to fine-tune the network pre-trained on the classification dataset ImageNet, which usually has better performance than a network trained from scratch. However, when pre-trained networks are used for network classification tasks, they tend to be translation-invariant and are implemented by down-sampling operations; however, down-sampling destroys the target's local texture information and conflicts exist [3]. To make matters worse, the network structure of the pre-trained network is difficult to change during the fine-tuning process during training. The sliding window mechanism for generating the anchor

© Springer Nature Switzerland AG 2020
D. Yu et al. (Eds.): WASA 2020, LNCS 12385, pp. 122–130, 2020.
https://doi.org/10.1007/978-3-030-59019-2_14

box has achieved excellent results [4]. However, for different detection targets, it is necessary to design anchor boxes of different shapes. The sliding window mechanism also has a fatal drawback, which is the huge amount of calculation, which is serious. It reduces the efficiency of the network and brings difficulties to the portability of the network.

This paper proposes a network structure for automatically designing anchor boxes from scratch. First, we use BatchNorm [5] to parameterize the optimization problem in the backbone network. We redesigned the network structure so that the network can be trained from scratch and effectively converged. Next, we used an automatically generated anchor box to solve the artificial prior factors. The network structure in this paper can effectively solve the problems of the pre-trained network and sliding window mechanism.

2 Model

Anchor [6] is the foundation of modern object detection. An anchor box can be represented by a vector quad (x, y, w, h), (x, y) for location, and (w, h) for shape. Suppose an object is drawn from image I, then its location and shape can be considered to follow a distribution with I as the condition, and its probability is $P(x, y, w, h|I)$. After decomposition, Eq. 1 can be obtained.

$$P(x, y, w, h|I) = \frac{P(x, y, w, h, I)}{P(I)} \tag{1}$$

After a series of deformations of Eq. 1, Eq. 2 can be obtained:

$$P(x, y, w, h|I) = P(x, y|I)P(w, h|x, y, I) \tag{2}$$

Two important information can be obtained from Eq. 2: (i) the specific area of the target in the image, and (ii) the scale and aspect ratio of the object are closely related to its location.

Based on this conclusion, we have drawn the network structure diagram shown in Fig. 1. The network generates a feature map I_1 through a custom SC-ResNet network from scratch, and then the anchor box generation module and the feature map adaptation module complete the detection task together. The network is named GasNet.

2.1 Non-pre-trained Backbone Network

Currently, pedestrian detection uses the ResNet [7] as a classification network for pre-training. As a result, the architecture is limited by the classification network and the network structure is not easy to modify. Without losing the generality of the training network, this paper adds BatchNorm to each layer structure of ResNet. BatchNorm makes the gradient descent more stable and smooth during the optimization process, thereby obtaining a larger search space and faster convergence speed. We call this network SC-ResNet. SC-ResNet makes up for the shortcomings of ResNet. It will get a more detailed introduction in Sect. 3.2.

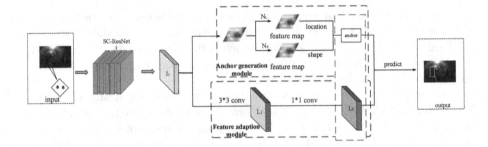

Fig. 1. The network structure diagram

2.2 Anchor Location Prediction

When predicting the location of the anchor, a probability map $P(\bullet|I_1)$ with the same size as the input feature map I_1 will be generated. The probability $P(x, y|I_1)$ on (x, y) is related to the coordinates $((x + \frac{1}{2})s, (y + \frac{1}{2})s)$ of the corresponding points, s represents the stride of the feature map, and its value $P(\bullet|I_1)$ represents the probability that the center of the object is located at that location.

$P(\bullet|I_1)$ is generated by the sub-network N_L. I_1 can obtain a probability value after a 1×1 convolution and a *sigmoid* function, which can balance efficiency and accuracy. In order to ensure the recall rate, we set a threshold ε_I to filter the possible locations of the object. Using the threshold can filter more than 90% of the area.

GasNet does not use predefined anchor box, so it needs to use some special techniques, otherwise it will reduce the training effect and even predict failure. We have introduced a way of binary label map to improve the accuracy of predicting the anchor location. Label 1 indicates that the anchor box location is valid, and label 0 indicates that the anchor box location is invalid. Since the location predicted by the anchor box is necessarily the location of the object, we can use a ground-truth map to generate the binary label map.

The prediction effect is best when the anchor box and the background box are completely coincident. When the anchor box is all located at the center of the background box and fewer anchor boxes are far from the center, the prediction effect is slightly less. We map the background box (x_g, y_g, w_g, h_g) of the truth map to the feature map (x_a, y_a, w_a, h_a), and use $R(x, y, w, h)$ to represent the center as (x, y) A rectangular area of size $w \times h$. In order to improve the initial IoU (Intersection over Union) of the anchor box and the background box, we divide the feature map into three regions:

1) Positive sample region: $TR = R(x_a, y_a, \sigma_1 w_a, \sigma_1 h_a)$ the central area of the object. The anchor box is located in this region, which is the target we are pursuing, and is marked as a positive sample.
2) Ignore region: $IR = R(x_a, y_a, \sigma_2 w_a, \sigma_2 h_a) - TR, \sigma_2 > \sigma_1$. The region obtained by removing the TR region from the background region, and the range of

this region is larger than the positive sample region. The pixels in this region are marked as ignore, directly ignore during training, reduce the amount of calculation.

3) Negative sample region: $FR = R(x_a, y_a, w_f, h_f) - R(x_a, y_a, w_a, h_a)$, where (w_f, h_f) represents the size of the feature, FR region is the area of the feature map minus TR and IR, this region is the area where the anchor box should not be placed, and this region is recorded as a negative sample.

2.3   Anchor Shape Prediction

After the anchor location prediction is completed, the anchor shape prediction can be performed. Given I_1, this branch will predict (w, h) at each location, then calculate IoU of the predicted shape and the nearest ground-truth box, choosing the box with the highest IoU, which is the final predicted result .

However, there is such a problem that the value range of (w, h) is too large, and it is difficult to predict directly. Therefore, the following transformations have been made: $w = kse^{\hat{w}}$, $h = kse^{\hat{h}}$. Among them, s is stride and k is the empirical coefficient, which is set to 10 in this paper. This branch is predicted by a sub-network N_S with $1 \times 1 \times 2$ convolution to get $\hat{w}$ and $\hat{h}$, and (w, h) is obtained by mapping. This method is different from the sliding window mechanism. A sliding window predicts a set of anchors at one location, but our method predicts only one dynamic anchor at one location, which can better capture extreme shape information such as small objects.

Since the w and h of anchors change dynamically, in order to obtain the most suitable shape for each anchor, in the process of calculating the IoU of the anchor box and ground-truth box to find the optimal w and h. We tried to use enumeration to calculate IoU, and found that the experimental results have reached our expectations. This approximation method can obtain the optimal IoU, and can be effectively embedded in the end-to-end network.

2.4   Loss Function

The loss function defined in this paper is as follows:

$$L = \lambda_1 L_{loc} + \lambda_2 L_{shape} + L_{cls} + L_{reg} \tag{3}$$

In this equation, L_{cls} is classification loss, L_{reg} is regression loss, L_{loc} is location loss, L_{shape} is shape loss, and weights $\lambda_1 + \lambda_2 = 1$. Moreover, L_{cls} is the standard classification loss, and the loss functions the other three parts are optimized.

In theory, the location distribution conforms to the mixed multivariate Gaussian function or Gaussian mixed function. In this paper, we assume that the location and coordinate are independent of each other, so we use a single-variance Gaussian function for computation. And finally we give the regression loss function:

$$L_{reg} = e^{-\alpha}(|x_g - x_e| - \frac{1}{2}) + \frac{1}{2}\alpha \tag{4}$$

In Eq. 4, x_e is the estimated bounding box location, x_g is the ground-truth bounding box location, $\alpha = \log(\sigma^2)$, and σ is the standard deviation of the Gaussian function.

Because the location of the anchor box is fixed, this paper only optimize (w, h), not (x, y, w, h), so the shape loss function is as follows:

$$L_{shape} = L_1(1 - \min(\frac{w}{w_g}, \frac{w_g}{w})) + L_1(1 - \min(\frac{h}{h_g}, \frac{h_g}{h})) \tag{5}$$

Where, L_1 is the standard regularization formula, w and h are the width and height of the anchor box respectively, w_g and h_g are the width and height of the ground-truth box respectively.

The location loss function uses focal loss [10], defined as follows:

$$L_{loc}(p_t) = -(1 - p_t)^\gamma \log(p_t) \tag{6}$$

Where, γ is the adjustable parameter, $\gamma > 0$, when the parameter $\gamma = 0$, the formula is the ordinary cross entropy function, and p_t is the probability obtained according to the ground-truth label mentioned above.

3   Experiment and Discussion

GasNet trains on dataset UMP2019, and fine-tuning the result model with stochastic gradient descent. The training batch size is 64, Subversion is 16, momentum is 0.9, weight decay is 0.001, and the maximum iteration number is 17,500. The experiment was based on the 64-bit operating system Ubuntu 16.04; The deep learning framework is Caffee, and four GeForce GTX 1080ti are used for training.

3.1   Dataset

At present, there are many public datasets for pedestrian detection, including INRIA and ETH, but these datasets are ground data, which are quite different from the mine environment and cannot be used for mine pedestrian detection. We use the dataset UMP2019, which was collected and produced by lab members in Taoyuan and Xinji Coal Mines. It includes different images such as dim, bright, blurred, dense crowd and hyperopia scenes. There are 18,450 images in total, including 14,760 training pictures, 1845 validation pictures, 1845 test pictures.

3.2   Backbone Network

The backbone network is the basis of GasNet, and its performance needs to be verified. We have proved through experiments that BatchNorm is effective in Resnet training from scratch.

Resnet is a classification network, and a detection network needs to be added to complete the experiment. We used learning rates of 0.001, 0.01 and 0.05, and added different components to the network to measure the network. Table 1 shows the experimental results. It can be seen that when the learning rate is 0.01 and 0.05, if the BatchNorm is not used, the network cannot effectively converge. Meanwhile, after using BatchNorm, we can use a larger initial learning rate to accelerate the training of the network. When the learning rate is 0.05, the network performance reaches a better result.

Table 1. BatchNorm validity experiment

Component	Learning rate = 0.001			Learning rate = 0.01			Learning rate = 0.05		
Pre-trained	√		√	√		√	√		√
BN (backbone)		√	√		√	√		√	√
AP (%)	70.1	74.3	79.0	NAN	77.2	79.9	NAN	78.1	80.2

After demonstrating the effectiveness of BatchNorm for a network trained from scratch, we modified ResNet and experimented with four network structures, and obtained the results in Table 2 after the experiment.

Table 2. Improved network structure comparison experiment

Network	ResNet-22	BN-ResNet-22-A	BN-ResNet-22-B	BN-ResNet-22-C
AP	84.1	86.3	88.6	89.5

ResNet-22 is a traditional ResNet network structure. BN-ResNet-22-A removes the max-pooling layer of ResNet-22, that is, the second down-sampling is cancelled; BN-ResNet-22-B changed the stride of the first convolution layer of ResNet-22 from 2 to 1, which cancels the first down-sampling operation; BN-ResNet-22-C replaces the first 7 × 7 convolution kernel of ResNet-22 with three 3 × 3 convolutions, compared with ResNet-22, the use of more redundant features will improve performance and AP increase 5.4%. The backbone network used in this paper is BN-ResNet-22-C, which ensures the robustness of the network and has the advantage of training from scratch.

3.3 Comparison

The premise of judging whether a network is effective is to detect whether the network can converge. Figure 2 shows the loss function curve of this paper. It can be seen that the convergence speed is very fast, and it has a gentle trend at the end, which ensures the effective convergence of the network.

We study the effectiveness of each part by changing different variables, including the backbone network, location prediction, shape prediction, and loss function. The results are shown in Table 3. By analyzing the results, we find that

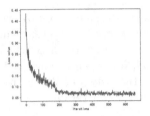

Fig. 2. Loss function graph

the shape prediction improves significantly. Although the location prediction improves less, they collectively form a branch structure, and its importance is reflected in the usefulness of generating sparse anchors. Meanwhile, the effect of using a custom loss function and the backbone network is also very obvious. Both designs effectively promote the convergence of the network.

Table 3. Effectiveness of network design

Component	GasNet				
Backbone?	√				
Location predict?	√	√			
Shape predict?	√	√	√		
Loss function?	√	√	√	√	
AP/%	96.3	94.4	92.8	90.8	89.5

Figure 3 shows the final experimental results of GasNet in different scenarios. It can be seen that the results are very good.

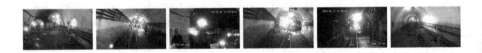

Fig. 3. Experimental result diagram

We counted 110 pictures among the 1845 pictures in the test set, and plotted the graph in Fig. 4. From the figure, we can see that our network has achieved excellent indicators in terms of accuracy and omission rate. Meanwhile, compared with Yolov1 [8], Faster R-CNN [6], SSD [9] and RetinaNet [10], GasNet has higher AP value.

In the case of the same recall rate, this paper calculates AP and detection speed to further verify the superiority of our network. As shown in Table 4, it is intuitively found that the AP value of this network ranks third, only lower than

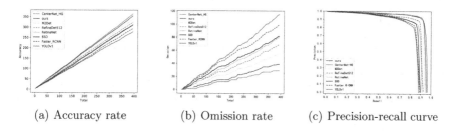

| (a) Accuracy rate | (b) Omission rate | (c) Precision-recall curve |

Fig. 4. Curve of accuracy and omission rates

CenterNet [11] and M2Det [12], but the speed of this network is higher than CenterNet and M2Det. Compared with CenterNet-HG, GasNet reduced AP by 0.8% and increased 17 FPS; GasNet decreased AP by 0.3% and increased 9 FPS compared to M2Det. The decline of AP has improved the detection speed, which is conducive to real-time mine pedestrian detection and an embedded platform applied to mine pedestrian detection.

Table 4. Experimental comparison table

Network	Backbone	Input size	Speed/(FPS)	AP/%
YOLOv1	GoogleNet	418×418	45.0	85.6
Faster R-CNN	VGG-16	$\sim 1000 \times 600$	7.0	87.8
SSD	VGG-16	300×300	46.0	89.3
RetinaNet	ResNet-101	$\sim 640 \times 400$	12.3	90.6
RefineDet512	VGG-16	512×512	22.0	93.9
M2Det	ResNet-101	512×512	15.0	96.6
CenterNet-HG	Hourglass-104	512×512	7.4	97.1
This paper	SC-ResNet-C	416×416	24	96.3

A high-quality anchor box is generated after branch prediction, as shown in Fig. 5. The examples of first three columns are RPN proposals. As can be seen from the figure, compared with the RPN method, the anchor box generation method in this paper has two advantages. First, the number of correct prediction boxes has increased, and second, the high-quality IoU is more useful.

Fig. 5. Proposal area comparison

4 Conclusion

This paper proposes a non-pre-trained mine pedestrian detection network based on automatic generation of anchors, which aims to solve mine pedestrian detection. In order to ensure the accuracy of pedestrian detection, the complexity of the network is high, and there is still a certain distance from the actual application on embedded platforms. Next, our research will focus on reducing the complexity of the network while ensuring the accuracy of detection.

Acknowledgments. This work was supported by Anhui Provincial Key R&D Program (201904d08020040) and National Key R&D Program of China (2018F YC0604404).

References

1. Lin, T.Y., Dollár, P., Girshick, R., et al.: Feature pyramid networks for object detection. In: Proceedings of the IEEE Conference on Computer Vision and Pattern Recognition, pp. 2117–2125 (2017)
2. Krishnamurthy, B., Sarkar, M.: Deep-learning network architecture for object detection. US Patent 10,152,655, 11 Dec 2018
3. Zhu, R., Zhang, S., Wang, X., et al.: ScratchDet: training single-shot object detectors from scratch. In: Proceedings of the IEEE Conference on Computer Vision and Pattern Recognition, pp. 2268–2277 (2019)
4. Anantaram, C., Kopparapu, S.K., Patel, C.R., et al.: Systems and methods for automatic repair of speech recognition engine output using a sliding window mechanism. US Patent 10,410,622, 10 September 2019
5. Ioffe, S., Szegedy, C.: Batch normalization: accelerating deep network training by reducing internal covariate shift. arXiv: Learning (2015)
6. Ren, S., He, K., Girshick, R., et al.: Faster R-CNN: towards real-time object detection with region proposal networks. In: Neural Information Processing Systems, pp. 91–99 (2015)
7. He, K., Zhang, X., Ren, S., et al.: Deep residual learning for image recognition. In: Proceedings of the IEEE Conference on Computer Vision and Pattern Recognition, pp. 770–778 (2016)
8. Redmon, J., Divvala, S.K., Girshick, R., et al.: You only look once: unified, real-time object detection. In: Proceedings of the IEEE Conference on Computer Vision and Pattern Recognition, pp. 779–788 (2016)
9. Liu, W., et al.: SSD: single shot multibox detector. In: Leibe, B., Matas, J., Sebe, N., Welling, M. (eds.) ECCV 2016. LNCS, vol. 9905, pp. 21–37. Springer, Cham (2016). https://doi.org/10.1007/978-3-319-46448-0_2
10. Lin, T., Goyal, P., Girshick, R., et al.: Focal loss for dense object detection. In: Proceedings of the IEEE International Conference on Computer Vision, pp. 2999–3007 (2017)
11. Zhou, X., Wang, D., Krahenbuhl, P., et al.: Objects as points. Computer Vision and Pattern Recognition. arXiv (2019)
12. Zhao, Q., Sheng, T., Wang, Y., et al.: M2Det: a single-shot object detector based on multi-level feature pyramid network. In: National Conference on Artificial Intelligence, vol. 33, no. 01, pp. 9259–9266 (2019)

Author Index

Printed in the United States
By Bookmasters